−1 l
20 men,
− 1 ler,
30 men
(10 min
30 min

1 ler.
|
|

Practical Dreaming

Awakening the
Power of Dreams
In Your Life

LILLIE WEISS, PH.D.

NEW HARBINGER PUBLICATIONS, INC.

Publisher's Note

Distributed in the U.S.A. by Publishers Group West; in Canada by Raincoast Books; in Great Britain by Airlift Book Company, Ltd.; in South Africa by Real Books, Ltd.; in Australia by Boobook; and in New Zealand by Tandem Press.

Copyright © 1999 by Lillie Weiss, Ph.D.
New Harbinger Publications, Inc.
5674 Shattuck Avenue
Oakland, CA 94609

Cover design and illustration © 1999 by Poulson/Gluck Designs
Edited by Andrew Liotta
Text design by Tracy Marie Powell

Library of Congress Catalog Card Number: 99-74367
ISBN 1-57224-164-0 Paperback

New Harbinger Publications' Website address: www.newharbinger.com

01   00   99
10   9   8   7   6   5   4   3   2   1
First printing

For Barry and Ez

Contents

Part 3   Questions and Answers

I thank Andrew Liotta for his skillful and respectful editing, which made my words and thoughts more clear and concise. I have appreciated his astute and insightful comments and the tremendous amount of work and effort he put into this endeavor. I also thank Kristin Beck, Catharine Sutker, and the rest of the people at New Harbinger Publications for their support, enthusiasm, and hard work on this book. I am grateful to Karen Wade for coming to the rescue and helping to get the manuscript ready so that I could send it to a publisher. Her technical skills, professionalism, and helpful attitude are deeply appreciated. I am indebted to the many people who have shared their dreams with me, particularly to Chuck who originally suggested writing this book and Anne who planted the seeds for the format.

Introduction

I am indeed a practical dreamer . . .
I want to convert my dreams
into realities as far as possible.

—Gandhi

Have you ever felt a certain way but didn't know why? Have you ever wished you could understand some of the reasons for your behavior? Do you sometimes have trouble assessing certain situations and wish you could see them more clearly? Have you ever felt stuck when you had a problem to solve or a decision to make? Have you ever had to come up with a creative idea but couldn't, no matter how much you thought about it? At those times, did you wish that you had a reservoir of internal wisdom that you could draw from whenever you wanted, a constant source of insight that would shed light on your problems and help you move on? You do! That source is your dreams, and they are available to you every single night when you go to sleep.

I have written this book for anyone seeking an improved awareness and self-knowledge in order to enrich his or her life. Dream analysis is a proven method for helping people learn about themselves. We all dream four to five times nightly and spend an average of four and a half years of our lives in the dream state, yet many of us ignore our sleep life and focus only on our waking thoughts and feelings. By disregarding our nighttime wisdom, we end up using only a fraction of our brain power when making decisions and problems.

To discount your dreams is to discount a part of yourself. When you use only a portion of your experiences in understanding yourself and others, you end up with a sort of tunnel vision. If you could learn to apply *all* of your mental faculties in your thinking, you would gain a perspective and clarity that you don't have when you approach situations with limited vision. Dreams shed light on these "blind spots" and provide you with an extra dimension of understanding. When you learn to use all parts of yourself instead of only those that you can access during the day, you make use of your full potential and approach life using all of your capacities instead of a limited few. If you can learn to understand and apply your internal, nightly wisdom, you can be happier, healthier, and more in control of your life.

Dreams allow you to access an untapped source of wisdom. Dreams are your own internal "wise man," whom you consult whenever you "sleep on a problem." Dreams can uncover your blocks and provide you with guidance on how to proceed in your daily life. You spend so many years of your life going to school and learning about many different subjects, yet you frequently ignore the one subject that is most important to you—yourself. Your dreams can help you understand yourself and the world around you. They let you tap into your creativity—your "higher selves." By drawing upon the wisdom of your dreams on a regular basis, you add an extra dimension to life and living, see situations more clearly and vividly, and operate with full, rather than partial knowledge. When you use *all* of yourself, you learn to treasure those precious four and a half years you spend in the dream state.

Over the years, I have spent hundreds of hours helping clients analyze their dreams and training other therapists in how to do dream analysis with their clients. I wrote my book *Dream Analysis in Psychotherapy* to teach therapists a method for getting at a dream's meaning. This method was developed by the late Dr. Hattie Rosenthal, to whom I owe much of my personal and professional growth and to whom that book was dedicated.

I have written this book to help you look at your dreams and decipher them without the help of an expert. Dreams have played such an important part in my life and in the lives of so many others with whom I have worked that I would like to share the tools that I have taught to therapists over the years. Most of my formal teaching of dream interpretation has been for therapists, although clients have frequently picked up the method on their own, by asking themselves the same questions that had been asked of them in their therapy sessions.

In this book, I will teach you a step-by-step method for understanding your dreams and applying them to your everyday life. The book consists of practical exercises to help you learn to use the basic steps in interpreting your dreams. Part 1 discusses the use of dreams in your daily life and suggests techniques for recalling and incubating dreams. Part 2 takes you through the different steps in the interpretive process.

Finally, part 3 answers some frequently asked questions about dreams.

If you can't recall any dreams at present, you are like most people. Dreams tend to be quickly forgotten. I will give you some specific suggestions for remembering dreams in chapter 3, but in the meantime, just keeping a small pad and pen by the bed to jot down your dreams is a start.

As you start paying attention to your dreams, you will learn more and more about yourself. We spend so many years in school studying the three R's but so little time getting to know the most important person in our lives—ourself. Dreams give you that inner self-knowledge. They let you discover your good parts and your bad parts, your strengths and weaknesses, so that you can integrate them or discard them as the case may be. They help you solve your problems and let you see things clearly; they serve as a stimulus for thought, and show you your feelings in Technicolor; you get to try out new experiences, and then say, "I didn't know I felt that way—that was so good" or "that was so powerful" or "that was so sad." And they are available to you every single night—four or five times a night!

By learning to interpret your own dreams, you will unlock strengths and talents you didn't know you had, uncover blocks to creativity as well as creative solutions to these blocks, tap into an endless reservoir of wisdom within you, and use your improved self-awareness to lead a more fulfilling and satisfying life.

Part 1

Understanding
Your Dreams

1

The Uses of Dreams in Everyday Life

If he would give as much thought to himself during the day as he does during the night, man might deepen his self-knowledge to the point where he could master his conflicts instead of being mastered by them.

—Calvin Hall

Several years ago I was planning a gathering for a large number of people and called up a caterer who had served a delicious meal at a dinner I had attended. We discussed the menu and made arrangements for her to cater my party. I was all set to send her a check when I had a disturbing dream. I dreamt it was time for the party, and the caterer did not deliver enough food. I was puzzled by this dream. The caterer had an excellent reputation. I had just been to a dinner she had catered, and the food was exquisite. What could possibly go wrong?

I decided to pay attention to what my dream seemed to be telling me. As I began to think about my interactions with this person, some pieces of information I had overlooked came to mind. When I originally called her to discuss the party, she said she would call back later that week to finalize the menu. However, she did not call back until the next week. I didn't pay attention to that detail at the time, dismissing it as unimportant. When she sent me the finalized menu, it was different from the one we had agreed on, but again I overlooked this information. My first thought when I had looked at this new menu was that it seemed pretty skimpy, but once more I discounted my initial impressions. Now my dream was telling me loud and clear, "PAY ATTENTION! This woman didn't deliver on her promise. What she delivered was not adequate." The information was there all along but I chose not to see it. I had already made up my mind about this caterer and didn't want any evidence to the contrary—evidence that could mean I'd have to find someone else, which would be a major inconvenience. But my dream was pointing out what I had chosen not to see: the problems with the caterer could result in a ruined dinner party.

> *All the things one has forgotten*
> *scream for help in dreams.*
> —Elias Canetti

Dreams as a Source of Knowledge

As you go about your daily life, you have many fleeting thoughts, impressions, and feelings that you don't pay attention to, either because you are too busy to notice or because you dismiss them as inconsequential. In your fast-paced life, you don't always have the opportunity to sit down and take stock of what is going on inside you. You may feel a momentary discomfort, a knot in the stomach or a sensation that you ignore and dismiss as unimportant, just as I had done when I discounted my own initial impressions about the menu. Dreams often consist of the thoughts and feelings you experienced during the day but which were not within your direct awareness. Dreams are nothing more than yourself "thinking" at night, churning over the information you took in during the day. You toss in all the ingredients—the random thoughts and images of the day—and let them simmer and settle in the cauldron of your mind at night.

Dreams Tell You What You Don't Know You Know

You have access to more than one kind of knowledge within you—the logical, conscious knowledge that is part of your daily awareness, and another type of knowledge that is just at the fringe of awareness, the things you "know" but haven't taken the time to process properly. You have different levels of awareness, and dreams often consist of those thoughts and feelings that you may not have been aware of in your waking state. Sometimes you dream of thoughts and feelings that you're already aware of, but the dream magnifies these experiences to bring certain details closer to your attention.

Colleen had been married for nearly seventeen years when she learned that her husband had been having an affair for the last ten years of their marriage. Her husband promised to discontinue the relationship, and life seemingly went back to normal. At least that's what Colleen wanted to believe. Colleen ignored her husband's long drives in the evening, his disinterest in lovemaking, and his extended absences when he'd drop the children off at activities. One day she had a dream that her husband was putting on cologne. "What do you think that means?" I asked her. "Well," she said, "he's certainly not putting it on for me!" Her dream was telling her what her conscious mind refused to acknowledge, what her unconscious mind knew all along.

What a clever, indirect way to call attention to something. The dream suggests, subtly, that something is amiss and then gently invites you to look at it. It gives a momentary hint— a whiff, in this case—of the problem. You may tell yourself you're unsure: "Did it or didn't it happen? Is it my imagination or isn't it?" Yet deep inside you *know*—you know the truth, and you can choose to look at it or to close your eyes to it.

> *It is at night ... that the mind is*
> *most clear, that we are most able to*
> *hold all our life in the palm of our skull.*
>
> —Brian Aldiss

What does it mean "to know"? There are two main ways of processing information, of knowing and understanding the world: logical, analytical, critical thinking (commonly referred to as "left brain" activity) and intuitive, metaphorical thinking ("right brain" activity). Both are needed to accurately perceive a situation, yet you often act as though only the *critical* (judgmental, logical) part of us is *critical* (important, necessary)—and the other way of knowing, superfluous and unnecessary. Dreams access this other way of knowing and show you that you know more than you're aware of.

> *A moments insight is sometimes*
> *worth a life's experience.*
>
> —Oliver Wendell Holmes

Dreams offer *in*sight—sight into the inner workings of your psyche. They help you look within yourself and understand your thoughts and actions. They can provide you with a level of self-consciousness and self-knowledge that you don't have available in your daily undertakings. Through your dreams, you can draw on both sides of the brain, becoming aware of your strengths and your weaknesses, your creative powers as well as your self-defeating behaviors. Dreams help you get in touch with your *entire* self, allowing you to think with your *whole* brain instead of only half of it. Dreams can uncover thoughts and feelings that were hidden. The new self-awareness you gain allows you to *choose* how to act, making you the master rather than the victim of your behavior.

> *Vision is the art of seeing things invisible.*
>
> —Jonathan Swift

Dreams Help You See More Clearly

You pick up knowledge through all of your senses, yet you may frequently discount any information you receive that does not fit with your preconceived notions—just as both Colleen and I ignored the various clues we received. Everyone has blind spots for certain aspects of life; dreams allow you to see these situations more clearly.

One of the most important features of dreams is their honesty; they show things the way they are. In your waking life, you may distort the information you receive because it is too painful, inconvenient, or socially unacceptable to face. The dream paints a picture—a vivid one—and invites you to look at yourself and your world more clearly, without your normal filters. The dream "tells it like it is," reminding you that sometimes the right brain is also the *right* brain. This self-awareness comes from deep within, and you can choose either to face this knowledge or to turn away from it.

> *Nothing is lost on him who sees.*
>
> —Thomas Moore

Most of us respect the knowledge we gain from analytical daytime thinking and dismiss the knowledge we get from our dreams. We go through life half-conscious, operating only at half-capacity, with only "half our brain." You can only be fully aware when you make use of all your knowledge. Then you can make decisions and solve problems based on accurate data, as opposed to the information you have access to during your waking moments—information that is frequently colored by your need to see things not as they are but as you wish them to be.

> *What is essential is invisible to the eye.*
>
> —Antoine de Saint-Exupery

Sarah had spent much of her life seeking her mother's approval and never got it. When her mother became ill with cancer, she flew home to visit her, longing for the warmth and closeness they might now provide for each other. The night before her trip she dreamt that her mother had her hands to her sides. Her dream helped prepare her for the inevitable disappointment she would experience and reminded her of the numerous instances when her mother had been cold and rejecting in the past. Even though Sarah "knew" this information about her mother, she still had blinders on, especially at this vulnerable time in her life. Her dream magnified that knowledge and served as a reminder for her of what her mother was really like.

> *In dreams we see ourselves naked and*
> *acting out real characters, even more*
> *clearly than we see others awake.*
>
> —Henry David Thoreau

Dreams Make You Aware of Your Vulnerabilities

I had a dream one night that I was being taken for a ride by a crazy cab driver. I feared for my life at first and then just worried about getting out of the cab and getting home. The next night I had a dream that a bus driver wouldn't let me on the bus. He was kinder and gentler than the crazy taxi driver in my first dream, so I wasn't scared; I was mad, and I didn't know why. Then it came to me: Why do I keep needing to be transported? Why do I depend on others to take me places? Why don't I have my own transportation? And how do I go about getting my own wheels so that I can ride on my own? The dreams alerted me that I was depending on others to take me places and leaving myself vulnerable in the process. If I didn't want to be "taken for a ride," I would have to rely on myself more. I also understood how I could rectify the situation so that I would feel more in control.

> *Within each one of us there is another*
> *whom we do not know. He speaks to us*
> *in dreams and tells us how differently he*
> *sees us from how we see ourselves.*
>
> —Carl Jung

Dreams can show you your childlike, infantile, dependent parts. They point out how you sabotage yourself and also provide you with the inner wisdom to change your behavior. Many times we act in ways that are not in our best interest. When you can recognize these self-defeating patterns in your dreams, you can "get in the driver's seat" and navigate your life to your satisfaction. We frequently dream about riding in some kind of vehicle. How are we traveling along the path of life? Are we going too fast? Too slow? Are we enjoying the ride? Do we have our lights on? Carol frequently had dreams that she was driving too fast and was going to have an accident. Her inner wisdom was telling her to slow down before she crashed.

> *I believe that dreams transport us through*
> *the underside of our days, and that if we*
> *wish to become acquainted with the dark*
> *side of what we are, the signposts are*
> *there, waiting for us to translate them.*
>
> —Gail Godwin

Dreams Show You How You Add to Your Problems

Your dreams can show you how your behavior may be contributing to your problems. Dreams sometimes even suggest a remedy. Louisa wondered why she had so few friends and what she was doing to turn them off. She dreamt that she had a disproportionately large head compared to the rest of her body. For the first time, she recognized her "big-headedness." By seeing herself more accurately, she could change how she behaved, and, she was hopeful, make more friends.

Sandra had a dream that she had a huge Christmas tree in her living room that interfered with a meeting she wanted to have. She moved to another room but it also had a Christmas tree that blocked everything in sight. No matter where she went, she couldn't get away from the Christmas tree. She felt frenzied and scattered, not her usual organized self. The message was clear: the Christmas tree was blocking what she wanted to do. Sandra decided to remove from her life some of the Christmas hassle that was keeping her from enjoying herself and doing the things that mattered to her.

Dreams Point Out Your Strengths

Dreams can make you aware of your assets, illuminating strengths you didn't know you had. You can, for example, see yourself performing feats you didn't know you could perform. A stutterer can dream of himself giving a brilliant speech. A person afraid of the water can find herself swimming. A man afraid of his boss can dream of telling him off. You can experience yourself doing things you didn't know you could. A young girl used to be terrified of dogs until she had a dream that she was petting a dog. The fear disappeared, and she recognized that she didn't have to be afraid anymore. A woman with a snake phobia dreamt that she was bitten by a snake. She was calm in the dream, not as panicky as she thought she might have been had the situation actually occurred.

When Lorna's husband asked her for a divorce, she thought that her world had fallen apart. She clung to him like a child clings to her mother. She was tearful, feeling helpless, dependent, and vulnerable. How would she manage without him? She dreamt she was standing beside Barbara Walters, a woman she saw as famous in her own right, an individual who was strong and able to express herself. As Lorna looked back at her life, she recognized how much she had come to lose her self-worth during her marriage. She had stopped expressing herself and let her husband make all the decisions. She had started to feel like a nobody, a feeling she did not have before she got married. Her dream reminded her of her "Barbara Walters Self"—the person who was, indeed, a "somebody," a person who could be strong and express herself. It reawakened her competent side and told her she could make it on her own, a reminder she badly needed at this time in her life.

Dreams Tap into Your Creativity

Many inventions and artistic creations arose from dreams. Billy Joel composed many beautiful tunes that he heard in his dreams. Other composers have talked about "the music of the Gods" that comes to them at night. William Styron's book *Sophie's Choice* was based on an image that appeared to him in a dream, as was Jacquelyn Mitchard's best-seller *The Deep End of the Ocean*. Mitchard had a detailed dream about an Italian family caught in an extraordinary crisis over their child. She knew their names, what they looked like, and what they would do. That dream was the basis for her novel.

> Have you ever slept on a problem and awakened the next morning with the solution? Elias Howe did, and he invented the popular sewing machine; Igor Stravinsky did, and he created "The Rite of Spring"...
>
> —Gayle Delaney

Inspiration for paintings has frequently come from dreams, where vivid pictures and brilliant colors often appear. Legend has it that the original concept of the sewing machine arrived in a dream. Buildings have been created in dreams. Some of our most remarkable thinkers—from Descartes to Einstein—have said their best ideas came while dreaming.

> *Dreams take us to levels that we*
> *would otherwise be afraid to strive for.*
> —Bill Beham

"Dental psychology," my husband said. "I had a dream that I was showing you this brochure about dental psychology, and it was colorful and brilliant and beautiful. I felt so enthusiastic and excited." Dental psychology? What *was* dental psychology? Although my husband and I are both psychologists, we had never heard of it, but since the dream was so vivid and exciting, we began talking about it. A light bulb went on. Of course! My husband, who specializes in the treatment of chronic pain, sees many individuals suffering from dental pain, and I treat women with bulimia who frequently have severe dental problems. In fact, I had often noted that dentists were sometimes the first health professionals to spot bulimia and could play a big role in its prevention. We had not done much with this information, even though we work in an office complex where we're surrounded by dentists. The resources were right under our noses—figuratively and literally—but we had not acted on them till the dream. We have subsequently written articles and planed workshops on the dental aspects of psychology.

Dreams as a Source of Experience

Cameron had never touched a woman in his life and never intended to. Because he was molested by a relative when he was a child, he had avoided all contact with females. At twenty-seven he had never even asked a woman out for a date, except once at a high school dance after pressure from his teacher. He had kept himself isolated, and despite his good looks and intelligence, he made certain he never got close to a girl. Since he avoided all social connections with females, he was never in a situation to practice affectionate behavior with them and learn that sexual activity could be pleasurable and not traumatic. One night he dreamt that he was kissing a girl whom he liked very much and was surprised at how good that felt. His dream allowed him to *experience* touching a female. The dream offered a safe place to rehearse for future situations, something he was unable or unwilling to do in his waking life.

Dreams Allow You to Rehearse Behavior

An old proverb states: "Tell me and I will forget. Show me and I may remember. Involve me and I will learn." Dreams *involve* us completely because, in essence, you live through the dream experience and can therefore learn from it. By being directly involved in the dream, by experiencing the emotions, Cameron could see for himself what kissing a girl felt like, and he could prepare for future experiences, something he eventually did in his waking life as well. The dream pointed out to Cameron strengths he didn't know he had and allowed him to try on behavior he was frightened of. His dream helped him practice and rehearse for the future.

Julie was frightened when she anticipated the surgery she was scheduled to have, especially when she heard that the pain would be comparable to labor pains during childbirth. Julie had never given birth and didn't know what that experience would be like. A few days before her surgery, she had a dream that she was giving birth and actually experienced herself having rather severe and prolonged pain. At the end of the dream she felt exhilarated to see her newborn baby. Her dream helped her experience giving birth—both the pain and the elation—and prepared her for her surgery. She now *knew* for herself that she would be able to withstand the pain and that she would feel relieved afterward. Her dream served as a rehearsal for the real event.

Dreams allow you to live out different situations and see for yourself what they feel like. By allowing you to live through the experience firsthand, they answer your question "How would I feel if. . . ?" A graduate student may have dreams of herself practicing in her field, rehearsing for a future role. A pregnant woman often dreams of feeding and nursing her child, preparing for her new identity. You can live through all kinds of situations and experiences and gain a truer understanding of what they feel like than you could get from any amount of research or advice. You experience the event— sights, sounds, smells, and all—so you truly know what it feels like. You can understand and learn from it, and feel prepared for the real thing.

You can try on behavior in dreams, without the real-life consequences. People who have been sober for years will frequently have dreams about going off the wagon and wake up relieved that they are still sober. The dreams remind them of what it would feel like if they slipped, only without the lasting damage that would ensue in their waking life. Ex-cigarette smokers who "would give anything for a smoke" can sneak a puff without the nicotine getting in their systems.

When you experience something in a dream, you can learn the lesson without having to be told—you feel it, sense it, experience it, in essence, you live it. Life's biggest lessons are learned when you experience the behavior and its aftermath. When you live out a situation, you can say "Hey, I can do this" or "I don't want to do this." Your experience is *real* to you even if it was "only a dream." And just like any experience, the dream becomes part of your life and your memories; you integrate it and incorporate it into the sum total of your experiences and knowledge, which you can tap into whenever you need it.

Dreams Help You Work Through Your Emotions

Did you ever wake up feeling exhausted, drained, refreshed, or exhilarated—knowing you felt that way because of all the emotions you let loose in your dream? Dreams bring out your feelings so you can experience them, get in touch with them, and ultimately get them out of your system. You may wake up feeling a sense of relief, having cried tears, vented anger, and shed sorrows in your sleep. Dreams can have a cathartic role (from the Greek word *katharsis*, meaning "to purge"). When you discharge your emotions, you feel purged, cleansed. One of the functions of dreams is to let out the pent-up feelings stored inside you and get rid of them. You may be able to feel something deeply in a dream, that your conscious mind will not allow you to feel in your waking state. When you purge these emotions, you wake up feeling satisfied that you finally told someone off or got something off your chest or shed tears of grief; you can release the tension inside you and feel a sense of peace.

Melanie's co-worker died six months ago. She was very stoic about his death, ignoring the pain she felt every time she went to work and didn't see him there. She didn't cry when she heard the news, and now she felt detached and removed from the whole situation. When she finally dreamt about him, she felt the grief well up inside her, and she was able to release all the pent-up emotions she didn't even know she had. Her dream allowed her to grieve her loss, something she had not been able to do when she was awake.

Glenda called me frantically late one evening. "I have to see you," she said. "I just watched a movie on television about a woman getting raped, and I need to see you as soon as possible." I made an appointment to see her first thing in the morning, but apparently she couldn't wait that long to get relief. That night she had a dream that she came to my office and expressed all the rage she felt about her own rape many years ago, a rage she had kept inside. She dreamt that she was in my office, and I told her, "You know what you need to do." She then started to vent her anger, screaming and yelling at the top of her lungs, smashing and breaking things, until she got all her fury out. She felt much better when she came to see me the next morning. Fortunately for both of us, the dream had enabled her to act out her rage, without having to break anything.

Dreams Release Your Nightmares

Dr. Hattie Rosenthal would congratulate people who had nightmares. "Bravo," she would say. "You have carried a nightmare inside you for a long time. Now you have the courage to face it." By discharging negative emotions, by confronting your worst fears, you can free yourself from them and not have them haunt you any longer. Your dreams allow you to purge your demons, to exorcise them and be rid of them. What's more, you can let out these feelings safely, without the consequences were you to let them out in your waking life. You can experience the satisfaction of hurting someone who has hurt you, without having to be punished for it. If you couldn't release these emotions at night, they might erupt like a volcano and overwhelm your waking life.

Dreams Provide What You Lack

Dreams often help you keep your emotional balance by providing you with experiences that make up for what you are missing during the day. What did prisoners who spent many years in a Nazi concentration camp during World War II under the most unbearable conditions dream about during their incarceration? In most cases, it wasn't about death or famine or the cruelty they saw in their day-to-day lives. No, many dreamt of loved ones and festive dinners and warmth and laughter—welcome relief from the severe deprivation of their harsh living conditions. It was as if their psyche was trying to make up for their suffering and knew that they needed to restore their psychological balance. They couldn't take any more suffering during the night since their daytime suffering was so intolerable. Their dreams helped them escape their waking conditions and tried to compensate for what was lacking during their waking lives.

Sometimes, people report that they have entertaining dreams where they wake up laughing. This usually happens to people during periods of intense work pressure, when they haven't taken any time to relax. It's as though their dreams are saying, "Hey, lighten up!" The lightheartedness and humor of the night can give you a break from the drab grayness of the day and help you restore your psychological equilibrium.

> *Existence would be intolerable*
> *if we were never to dream.*
>
> —Anatole France

Dreams Maintain Your Psychological Balance

Can you function normally without dreaming? What would happen if you weren't allowed to dream? Some researchers (Dement 1960) asked themselves these questions and conducted dream deprivation studies where they woke up subjects every time they were in REM state (REM is an acronym for rapid eye movement). Research in sleep laboratories has shown that we do most of our dreaming during cycles of rapid eye movements, which occur nearly every hour and a half (Dement and Kleitman 1957a, 1957b). In the dream deprivation studies, the researchers did not keep subjects from sleeping, only from dreaming. In other words, they woke them up during REM periods, not during non-REM sleep. When subjects were not allowed to dream, they showed symptoms of psychological distress similar to an anxiety attack. The dream-deprived subjects had memory problems and difficulty concentrating, and they became anxious, irritable, and tense. When they went back to sleep after being awakened, they tried to make up for lost REM time by going to REM faster and having longer and more frequent REM periods. What's more, their psychological symptoms disappeared once they made up the lost REM sleep. None of the control subjects who were awakened during non-REM periods showed these psychological disturbances.

The results are even more dramatic when people are deprived from dreaming for a very long time. In these experiments (Dement 1964), the subjects experienced extreme distress, some became paranoid and displayed psychotic symptoms, and some even started to hallucinate! Again, when these subjects were allowed to dream again, they made up for lost REM time, and their symptoms disappeared! These results suggest that we *need* our dreams, and that some people can actually become disturbed and show psychotic symptoms if they are not allowed to dream. It seems our dreams keep us sane and balanced.

Other researchers (Zarcone et al. 1968, Gillin and Wyatt 1975) wondered, "If normal people start to hallucinate when they are not allowed to dream, what would happen if you deprived individuals of their dreams who were *already* hallucinating?" When they tested actively hallucinating schizophrenic patients, they found that these individuals did not seem to need the REM state and did not make up for lost REM time when deprived of dreams. The researchers reasoned that since the schizophrenics were already halluccinating during the day, they did not need to do so at night. It seems that "nighttime hallucinations" prevent daytime hallucinations.

Other studies have shown how your dreams help you retain your emotional stability and allow you to cope better in your daily life. In a study of pregnant women (Winget and Kapp 1972), those women who had the most anxiety dreams during their pregnancy had the least prolonged labor, and those who had the least anxiety dreams had more difficult and anxious births. By working through their fear in their dreams, they were able to rid themselves of it and therefore feel better prepared to face a challenging situation.

> *Dreaming permits each and every one of us to be*
> *quietly and safely insane every night of our lives.*
>
> —William Dement

You can probably recall instances when you had dreams the night before a stressful event. You have to teach a class, give a speech, or take an exam the next day, and you have dreams that everything goes haywire: your students don't show up, you forget your lines, everyone laughs at you, and all your fears and anxieties—anxieties you may not even be aware of—come to pass. These "Murphy's Law" dreams—when everything that could possibly go wrong, does go wrong—are very helpful. They allow you to discharge your feelings of nervousness and apprehension so that you can face the real-life situation feeling more composed and prepared. When you rid yourself of your "garbage" at night, it doesn't trouble you as much during the day, and you are able to relax and cope better with new situations.

Dreams as a Source of Wisdom

How often have you pondered over a problem and decided to "sleep on it"? When you are consciously working through something in your mind and can't come to a conclusion, dreams often provide answers. As I was writing this chapter, for example, I puzzled over how much material—including my own dreams—to put in. I had a dream that I was decorating my yard, and there was a dirty bathrobe on the clothesline, among many other objects, and I was trying to decide which ones to make room for. I remember thinking I don't need to display everything I have, and the yard doesn't have to be symmetrical. I decided to remove the dirty bathrobe. The dream helped me figure out how much of the old stuff to use in this chapter and how much to put away. I decided I didn't need to "air my dirty laundry" or to include all the material I had or even to give equal time to all parts.

Dreams Help You Solve Problems

When you are too tired or frazzled to think clearly, dreams can provide you with solutions. Karen could not remember where she put her keys. After sleeping on the problem, she was able to see where she had left them. We can solve all kinds of knotty problems in our dreams; anything from how to get the car working, to how to manage our finances. Dreams can help on any issue, large or small. It could be something as simple as planning a menu or as important a decision as whether or not to take a job, or how to cope with a parent, spouse, or lover.

In fact, there is a process called *dream incubation* (which I will describe more fully in chapter 3) in which you can try to dream about a specific problem you need help with. Just as a hen sits on its eggs and waits for them to hatch, you can sleep on a problem and wait for a solution to emerge. Experts agree that there are several stages to most creative ideas. When you are actively working on a problem, you consciously collect information related to it. Then you release your conscious hold on the problem and turn your attention elsewhere. During this period of time when you are not consciously working on a problem—the incubation stage—ideas can germinate and start to take form. Many researchers feel that incubation is the most critical stage in coming up with creative ideas.

> *It is a common experience that a problem*
> *difficult at night is resolved in the morning*
> *after the committee of sleep has worked on it.*
>
> —John Steinbeck

Dreaming provides you with that free-flowing mind state that is essential in making new connections. In this state, ideas can germinate, unrestricted by the mind's conscious restraints. In dreams, you loosen the rocks and blocks lodged deep in the crevices of your mind, and as a result you can discover new ways of looking at a problem, sometimes even getting a sudden glimpse of the answer. Dreams sometimes have "moments of clarity," when a fresh light is shed on an issue, so that you can see it in a whole new way.

Dreams Are Your Internal "Wise Man"

Linda did not know what she should do about her marriage of nearly fifteen years. She and her husband had separated for the third time, and she wondered whether she should try again or if her marriage was beyond repair. She looked to her dreams for guidance. That night, she dreamt there was a big hole in her kitchen floor. Her husband wanted to put a patch on the hole but she thought to herself, "You can't do that. You need to take the whole thing out and start from scratch." Linda's inner wisdom confirmed what she probably knew: she couldn't just keep patching up her marriage. The hole was too big to mend; it was time to leave and start anew.

> *Nothing said to us, nothing we can*
> *learn from others, reaches us so deep*
> *as that which we find in ourselves.*
>
> —Theodore Reik

Shirley also incubated a dream to shed light on her marriage. She was unhappy and didn't know why. Her husband was a good provider, faithful and reliable; yet something was missing. Why couldn't she be content? What was wrong with her that she couldn't appreciate him? She had a dream that the heating element in her blanket was not working. The blanket was an apt metaphor for her husband—her "security blanket"—who was devoid of warmth. The dream made her aware of what was wrong in her relationship and helped her see her problem in a new light. She no longer felt there was something the matter with her for not appreciating what she had.

You can also incubate dreams about problems at work. Lydia had an anxious feeling in the pit of her stomach when she thought about the new project she was asked to take on. The work sounded exciting, and she could use the extra money, but she had worked for that company before—with disastrous results. This company was very chaotic, much like a dysfunctional family. She had been assured she could do the work at her home, having only minimal contact with the organization; but she still felt uneasy. The night before the meeting in which they would iron out the details, she had a dream about a sick cat who was throwing up red dye and staining the rug. As the cat rolled on the white carpet, it kept smearing the dye and making a bigger and bigger mess. The cat couldn't be contained. Lydia recognized that the sick cat represented the sick organization that would affect and color everything within its realm. Her dream told her that the sickness would affect her even if she worked from her home. Because of this realization, she refused the offer.

You can even seek philosophical advice in dreams. Bill thought to himself before he went to sleep, "Why is there so much evil in this world?" He asked the same question again in his dream, and heard a voice answer loud and clear: "Do something about it!"

The process of asking dreams for guidance and coming up with answers is not as mysterious as it seems. Your dreams, since they access details that may have escaped your conscious attention, can provide an added wisdom, perspective, and clarity that you do not always have access to in waking life. Most important, *the wisdom comes from you*—it comes *from within*—and you can heed that inner voice, knowing that it tells it like it is.

Dreams are your allies, your friends, a constant source of wisdom. Dreaming is like putting on your thinking cap at night. It's like having your own therapist inside you, drawing upon your inner wisdom in order to guide you in the right direction.

Dreams Are Messages from Yourself to Yourself

Probably the most important aspect of dreams is the messages they provide. The dream message comes from your own knowledge, your own inner wisdom. Dreams often carry a message suggesting what to do or what not to do. A dream is like a story, and the dream message is the moral of the story:

the lesson the dream is trying to teach the dreamer. The message says, "If you do this, this will happen" or "If you don't do this, that will happen." In your dreams, you can see for yourself what would occur if you acted in such and such a manner. The dream points out a specific issue, and you can choose to ignore it or to act on it.

> *We are asleep with compasses in our hands.*
> —W. S. Merwin

The dreams in this chapter have all had messages for the dreamer. A dream says to me, "Look, if you depend on others to take you for rides, you might end up feeling a lack of control or being taken for a ride." It advises a self-important woman, "Hey, you're big-headed!" It tells Linda, "The hole in your marriage is too big—you cannot patch it up." It cautions Lydia, "If you work for a sick organization, it will color everything you do." *And at the same time the dream reveals the problem, it suggests the solution embedded in it.* It shows me that the way to avoid being taken for a ride is to get my own wheels. It tells the big-headed woman that the means to make friends is to stop inflating her self-importance. It confirms for Linda that she needs to leave the marriage and start anew. It illustrates for Lydia that she cannot escape the mess in the organization, and that the only solution is to stay away.

The dream message usually appears in disguised form, packaged in unintelligible, obscure language. Understanding what the dream is trying to teach you—deciphering the dream message—is simply translating that language into a form you can understand.

> *Dreams are our truest friends: they entertain us, they encourage us, they educate us, they soothe us, and most importantly, they free us.*
> —Bill Beham

Summary and Review

Dreams consist of thoughts and feelings you experienced during the day but which were not within your direct awareness. They tell you what you don't know you know. They help you see more clearly, bringing to your attention strengths and talents you didn't know you had, as well as pointing out how you might be undermining yourself. By *experiencing* behavior in your dreams, you can rehearse for future behaviors and release pent-up emotions. In addition, studies have shown that dreams can help you maintain your psychological balance. Your dreams also assist in solving problems and making decisions. They are messages from yourself to yourself and derived from your own inner wisdom.

Can you think of examples from your own dreams where they have allowed you to see a situation more clearly? Have you ever "slept on a problem" and found clarity upon awakening? Have you ever acted on the information you received from dreams? As you start paying attention to your dreams, you will find how useful they can be to you in your everyday life.

2

The Language
of Dreams

*Dreams say what they mean but they
don't say it in daytime language.*

—Gail Godwin

Dreams have their own language. A dream may seem nonsensical at first, but as you learn to decipher its foreign language, it becomes more understandable. As you learned in the last chapter, a dream is a message you send to yourself. The message sometimes comes in obscure, unintelligible language, and you can choose to look at it or to reject it. Dream interpretation is a translation from one language to another, from one level of consciousness to another, transposing your nighttime associations into more intelligible daytime language. Dream analysis is translating the language of your inner world into that of your outer world.

> *The dream-work . . . does not think,*
> *calculate, or judge in any way at all;*
> *it restricts itself to giving things a new form.*
>
> —Sigmund Freud

Dream Language

Dream language is "right brain" language—intuitive, imaginative, metaphorical, fluid, free-flowing, and creative. It is a language where connections are easily made, a language of fantasy without the constraints of daytime logic. In dreams, things happen that are not possible in waking life: you can be an actor and an observer at the same time, you can fly, you can take seconds to do what takes days, and you can be in several places at once. The logic of dreams is so different from everyday logic that it can be difficult to describe a dream in ordinary words.

A dream is witty and clever and has its own rules. It is a language of puns, of metaphors, and of humor. Once we learn to understand this playful and delightful language, we can use it to help us in our daily life.

What does this language look like? Here are some of its characteristics:

- Dream language is visual.

- Dream language is concrete.

- Dream language is experiential.

- Dream language is symbolic.

- Dream language is metaphorical.

- Dream language is playful.

- Dream language is creative.

- Dream language is economical.

Dream Language Is Visual

A dream is a picture story. It is like watching a movie playing in your head. Some dreams are like long movies with complicated plots; others are made up of snippets and fragments, or even a single isolated image. Dreams are like photographs, bringing with them a rush of memories and emotions, capturing the gist of the moment.

> *Me: "There is something wrong with my life and I don't understand what it is."*
>
> *Dream: "Look, I'll draw you a picture."*
>
> —Hugh Prather

If a picture is worth a thousand words, a dream is worth a thousand pictures. Once you get beyond the confusion and understand its language, a dream becomes a Kodak moment of clarity. Some of the images become indelibly etched in your mind. I sometimes forget what someone has told me or even what I had for breakfast that morning, but I almost never forget a powerful dream image. One of my clients dreamt of herself as "a puppy frozen in ice." This image was more vivid and moving than anything her conscious mind could tell me about herself. An image I will never forget occurred in a dream that a client had about a man she was considering marrying, but whom she had doubts about. She dreamt of "a purple sponge"—a royal sponger—an excellent word-picture of her boyfriend who was sponging off her royally. A wife's dream of her husband making meatloaf for her when she was a vegetarian told me more about their relationship than hours of therapy could have.

Another woman's fear that her fiancé would kill himself by smoking was depicted in this dramatic image:

> I had a nightmare that I went to a concert with my fiancé, and then he got electrocuted and turned into a cigarette butt.

A friend of mine had the following dream when she was house-hunting while pregnant:

> I dreamt that I was about to lay an egg and I couldn't find a nest.

A dream image—"gun hidden in a loaf of Syrian bread"—paints a vivid word-picture of the violence hidden under the guise of nourishment for a woman which was having difficulty with her family, which was of Syrian origin.

Dream Language Is Concrete

Dreaming is a picture language, using concrete images to represent thoughts and feelings. In this way, dreams are like movies. A movie doesn't tell you two people are in love but shows scenes of them holding hands, kissing, and looking misty-eyed at each other. A movie doesn't announce that two people are married but shows their wedding bands. Similarly, in dreams we use concrete pictures of narrative events— scenes— to depict ideas. Instead of dreaming of a commitment, you might dream of a wedding band. You might dream of a church or a cross as opposed to a mention of religion. A child might portray your childish side, while Mother Teresa represents your saintly aspects, or Picasso represents your artistic traits.

Dream Language Is Experiential

Just as causal relationships and complex ideas are difficult to express in a concrete picture-language, so are feelings. People don't dream of love or passion in the abstract; they *experience* the feelings. Dreams go further than showing you: they *involve* you. You are at once observer and actor. You feel and experience the pain, the joy, the sorrow, and the fear. And when you live through an event, you know it in a way that no amount of reading or studying could ever explain.

Some of your most vivid moments occur in dreams, and the emotions can carry over to your waking life: you wake up feeling love for the person you dreamt of, or the exhilaration of having accomplished a goal in your dream. John had one of the most moving experiences in his life when he dreamt that his father had come and kissed him on the face. The overwhelming love and emotion he felt was difficult to describe or explain. That moment stayed with him and changed him. Dream experiences affect us and remain with us. Experience is the best teacher.

Dream Language Is Symbolic

In the picture-language of dreams, symbols are the alphabet. Dreams use symbols to represent different thoughts and ideas. A symbol stands for something else by virtue of the two having a common feature. For example, a snake could be symbolic of a devious person because they both attack without warning. A lion could represent anger because both roar. A dog could stand for loyalty, laziness, or affection, depending on the trait it shares with the object or idea it represents. The purpose of dream interpretation is to find the common trait that links symbol and object, and see where it applies to your waking life.

All Symbols Are Individual to the Dreamer

A puppy could mean affection or detachment, inconvenience or playfulness, depending on how the dreamer views puppies. *There are no common or universal symbols.* We cannot go to a dream dictionary and look up, for example, "San Diego," to discover its meaning.

To some, San Diego can represent sun and fun; to others, it can mean bad memories. *To understand the meaning of a dream, you have to define the symbol and get its particular association for you.* The shared traits of the symbol and its object form the bridge between the dream language and your waking language. I will discuss this in more detail in the chapters on interpretation.

In my classes, I frequently ask students to define common symbols. Take a couple of minutes and write down what the word "cat" means to you. In a class of thirty people, I have gotten thirty different definitions. Here are a few of them:

- A cat is an independent creature who is bright and resourceful.

- A cat is cuddly and affectionate.

- A cat is catty and vicious.

- A cat is a parasite—I can't stand cats.

- A cat is funny and quick.

- A cat is sneaky and slimy.

As you can see, the meaning of a symbol is unique to the person describing it.

I attended a dream workshop many years ago where a person shared her dream and the different participants gave their associations to it. The dreamer had dreamt she was in a restaurant. It was one I was not familiar with, but it apparently was part of a common chain on the East Coast, where the conference was being held. Definitions of the restaurant ranged from "a dump or dive" to "a pleasant family place" to "one of the most romantic places to be." The responses told me more about the people interpreting the dream than about the dreamer.

The same point was humorously made in a column by Ann Landers. A man had written her that he dreamt he was naked and walking down Wilshire Boulevard in Los Angeles. When he went into a fashionable restaurant for dinner, no one noticed his nudity, but the hostess told him she couldn't seat him without a necktie. After the column ran, eleven thousand "experts" from all over the country wrote her with an interpretation of his dream. The responses included seeing the dreamer as a closet exhibitionist, a sex maniac, a fallen Catholic, a free-loader, or simply a stupid man. They recommended calling the police, turning to Jesus, finding a new girlfriend, and even getting to know the hostess better. The interpretations told more about the people interpreting the dream than about the dreamer!

Since symbols are unique to the dreamer, *no one can interpret your dream for you.* Nobody can look at your dream and tell you what it means, because the symbols are yours, derived from your own unique experiences, associations, and memories, and only *you* know what they represent. Your mind takes your daytime associations and gives them new forms in your dreams.

Everything in a Dream Is Symbolic

In dreams, both the *objects* and the *actions*—the nouns and the verbs—are symbolic. For example, if I dream that my red sports car is crashing, both "red sports car" and "crashing" are symbols. The red car could represent an aspect of me, and crashing could represent an accident or a loss of control. If I dream that I am going up in an elevator, it may reflect an elevation in mood. If I dream that I am sleeping, it may represent being oblivious to something. Being hot or cold in a dream could represent how I feel in my relationships.

Since everything in a dream is symbolic, you need to analyze *everything* in the dream, every detail, before you can arrive at a thorough interpretation. It pays to go through a dream patiently and not to dismiss any details as insignificant. Every detail is important in dreams, no matter how trivial it may seem when you first look at it. Sometimes people overlook details that don't fit with the rest of the dream. If there is something out of order—something that doesn't conform to everyday logic—you might think you should correct it, forgetting that it is already "correct" in dream language. The detail is there for a reason, *otherwise you would not dream it.*

If you are unable to interpret a certain detail in a dream, it is better to leave it partially interpreted than to force an incorrect interpretation on it. Even if you only understand a part of the dream, you get something valuable out of it. A later dream or further thought might help you clarify the hidden meaning. In the long run, it's worth your while to learn to do dream interpretation accurately and thoroughly. In order to do this, you must first learn the alphabet and vocabulary of your dream language.

Dream Language Is Metaphorical

A common trait of dream language is that it expresses metaphors literally. For example, an image of finding a key could stand for having the "key to a problem." A picture of oneself in the dark could mean being "left in the dark" or unaware of an issue. A concrete image of being asleep while driving could represent being "asleep at the wheel" or not paying attention. Other examples of concrete images that depict metaphors include being in the driver's seat, being lost, flying high, being in muddy water, and so on.

Sometimes images are used to symbolize specific expressions that are not quite so obvious. When the actions in a dream are not immediately understandable on a symbolic level, it is often a good idea to look for these literal expressions in the dream images since dreams often use concrete pictures to depict the expressions that are part of your daily vocabulary. For instance, dreams could depict "egg on my face," "a bee in my bonnet," "the rug pulled out from under me," "spilling the beans," "having a screw loose," "a lot of baloney," or any number of images depicting metaphors or idioms. Dreams take these verbal expressions literally. Annie pictured her teacher feeding her with a spoon, her wish for the material to be "spoon-fed" to her. She dreamt of "doing back flips" to impress a man she was interested in. When he asked someone else out for a date, she had a dream of him "slipping through my fingers."

Another way dream language conveys complicated ideas is through punning. A woman dreamt of a man named "Cando" (pronounced *can-do*) to represent someone helpful. A newcomer to Arizona who was feeling hopeful about it had a dream about a map of the state which was called "Hopiland"—a land of Hopi Indians and a land of Hope. Names of people can be words spelled backwards, so that someone named "Evol" could stand for love. Sometimes words that sound alike are substituted for other words. For example, an image of being inside a "roll" of bread could refer to getting into a "role," an image of an "ant" could refer to an "aunt," and so on. Names can also be treated literally. "Stew" could stand for "Stu" or a glass of sherry could represent "Sherry."

Dream language communicates much like a person doing charades: the player tries to depict a title of a song or movie without speaking and so must either act it out or portray something that sounds like it. Playing with the sound of words is one of the characteristics of dream language. Remember to listen for these word-games when a name, word, or phrase in a dream seems to defy explanation.

Dream Language Is Playful

When I wrote my first book on dreams for my colleagues, a mentor I hold in high esteem wrote me a letter mentioning that I had neglected to include an important aspect of dreams—dream humor—and sent me some examples, a few of which I will include here. The first was dreamt by a woman who used to be an English major:

> I was trying to dislodge a coffee pot that was wedged in the V of a tree trunk. As much as I tried, I could not budge it. In anger I hollered at the coffee pot: "Out, out, damned spout!"

A psychology graduate student had the following dream before taking an important exam:

> All the candidates were in the same room. I was one of the last to get my exam but I could see that the others had started to write as soon as they got their questions, so I concluded that it must be an easy exam. I was astounded to discover that the entire exam consisted of one question: "Write the word 'how', as many different ways as you can in Greek." Naturally I discovered that I was the only person in the whole room who did not know Greek—the others were Greek priests, classic scholars, etc. In other words, the exam was "all Greek to me."

A man with a big libido and good sense of humor related a dream to me about his wife, who didn't like to get up early in the morning and who didn't share his sex drive:

> It was very early in the morning, and my wife was performing a sexual act on me. In the background, someone is singing "To Dream the Impossible Dream."

A woman who had a very low opinion of an ex-boyfriend dreamt he had a distended colon. She figured that this was the dream's humorous and polite way of referring to her ex-boyfriend as an "asshole." She thought the dream was entirely correct.

> *An artist is a dreamer consenting*
> *to dream of the actual world.*
>
> —George Santayana

Dream Language Is Creative

The mental agility in dreams is hard to deny. Letting go of our conscious control can result in some wonderful images and fantasies. Even individuals who are not ordinarily creative have very ingenious dreams. A dream is the inner artist at play. We get scenes and plots from the film director and actor, landscapes and portraits from the photographer and painter, poetry from the writer, humor from the comedian, and wisdom from the philosopher. I am as amazed by the clever plots and metaphors in dreams as I am when I watch a good movie or play, read a book or hear a joke. Where does all this creativity come from? It all arises from the same source—your inner wisdom and creativity. When the mind is given free reign and allowed to play, it gives birth to innovative and clever ideas.

> *We are the music-makers,*
> *We are the dreamers of dreams.*
>
> —Arthur O'Shaughnessy

Dream Language Is Economical

Dreams frequently combine several objects or ideas into one image. Psychologists call this process *condensation*. Condensation provides a shortcut for saying something. For example, an aunt can symbolize the entire family, or a single co-worker can stand for everyone at the office.

Dream language can condense several complex ideas into one image. A woman dreamt of a license plate that read "San Diego + 3"—a shorthand way of depicting her marriage: three years since her honeymoon in San Diego. A person about to undergo surgery had a dream about "a butcher with a limp." In this image, she condensed several ideas. The butcher represented her surgeon, and the limp combined her fears: that he would be incompetent and that he would leave her deformed.

Bob, a widower, was contemplating remarriage but was unsure. He had a dream about "a map that when you turn it around is really a racing form." He incorporated several ideas into one image. The racing form represented something he did for fun, gambling, and a map was something that could lead the way. In one image he indicated that he was looking for guidance in his relationship, that the relationship was a gamble, and also lots of fun.

Lorna was trying to decide whether to recycle some old presents to give her nephews for Christmas. She dreamt that she gave her nephews two pink Halloween pumpkin bags. The image condensed two ideas: wrong sex and wrong holiday, letting her know that these were inappropriate presents.

*Nothing so much convinces me
of the boundlessness of the human
mind as its operations in dreaming.*

—William Benton Clulow

Dream Logic

Just as dream language has its own words in the form of symbols, it also has its own grammar. Dreams operate under different rules than those that govern waking life. You can transform images in dreams, you can fly, you can be two people at the same time. Dream language transcends everyday logic just as dream physics defy the natural laws of gravity and the constraints of time and space.

Dreams use a number of devices to deliver their message, just as movies use flashbacks, close-ups, and special effects to tell their story. These devices, called *dream mechanisms*, are tools used to bring material to your attention in this visual language. I've already discussed the most common dream mechanism, *symbolism*, which uses visual images to represent abstract objects and actions. Dreams use other processes to illustrate points, and as you begin to understand these dream processes and how they work, dream logic starts to make sense.

Omission

Dreams call attention to issues in subtle ways. Rather than spelling out the obvious, they hint at it and let the conscious mind decipher the message. One of the processes operating in dreams is that of *omission*. By omitting an important detail, the dream calls attention to it. Kathy had a dream in which the bed she shared with her husband had only three legs. This detail would have been easy to overlook in order to fit it in with everyday logic; but *wait!* It is precisely the missing leg that gives the clue to the dream. Something was missing in her marriage bed; the missing leg provides the key to the dream's meaning.

To properly analyze a dream, you must pay attention to what is omitted. A dream might have a beginning and an end, but no middle. A building could have three stories, but you can only recall the top and bottom floors. A table can have three legs. A house could have no living room. A mother of four children can dream of only three. Sometimes you can focus so much on what *is* there, you miss the crucial detail that *isn't*.

Exaggeration

Although a dream can call attention to something by omitting it, more frequently a dream highlights a problem by exaggerating it to such a degree that it makes the dreamer aware of its absurdity. A young woman dreaming she is completely alone in New York City can recognize the exaggeration in her dream, which pokes fun at her solitary tendencies. Exaggeration is like a close-up in film; by magnifying, intensifying, and dramatizing an image, dreams call attention to it and show us how absurd our thinking can be.

Alma had this dream after her boyfriend berated her for being late:

> I dreamt I had the bubonic plague. I was going to have surgery to remove it. I remember having kept the surgeons waiting.

This is dream humor at its best, telling her "Lighten up! It's not as though you have the bubonic plague!" The dream gives its message by calling attention to the absurdity of the situation. A woman obsessed with her weight had the following dream:

I ask a friend to go out, and she says to me, "I won't go out with you because you have put on thirty pounds." I think to myself, "That's really stupid."

By exaggerating and dramatizing her fears, she could see the absurdity of her thinking.

Numbers

The use of *numbers* in a dream is no coincidence, and they are often an important characteristic of the object described. In the example given previously of the license plate "San Diego + 3," the number three reflected the number of years of marriage.

Lauren dreamt she was trying to hide money from some people. They found it anyway and took a hot metal ring and burned her on five parts of her body. When we explored the dream together, she recognized that she was feeling tortured because of a new policy at work where they were taking money out of her paycheck—*for five pay periods!*

A woman who had cheated on her husband suspected that he might be cheating on her with a woman in another city. She had the following dream:

I dreamt that my husband was telling me that he had been attracted to Bess but he hadn't acted out like I had. He stopped it in time, unlike myself. He said he had only gone to Los Angeles to see her eight or nine times.

The numbers here are significant: "eight or nine times" were the number of times *she* had strayed. Whereas consciously she believed his denials of an affair, she knew at another level that he would only be doing what she had done in the past.

Another unique dream feature is the *fusion of images*, when two things are merged together in a dream. A client of mine had a hard time describing a person in his dream: "It was my uncle—or was it Tom? I don't know. It was a combination, I think." No wonder people have a hard time using ordinary words to describe what happens in dreams! But in the dream it all makes perfect sense. Fusing two images together is the dream's shorthand way of combining characteristics of both characters. For example, Tom and my uncle could both be angry men, or they could simply represent different aspects of the dreamer.

Transformation

Have you ever had a dream where one character suddenly changed into someone else? "It was me—and then it was my best friend, Scarlet." This is a transformation of images. In the dream it all holds together and seems totally logical, but as you wake up and try to retell it in ordinary language, it seems absurd. "It started out to be Joan and then somehow it turned into the cleaning lady and then . . ." When one person changes into another, it may represent a transformation or growth of one aspect of a person to another. For example, Joan could reflect a childish, immature part of you, while the cleaning lady could represent a more mature aspect.

Projection

"I dreamt that a friend of mine was drinking himself to death, and I was telling him to stop," Joe, an alcoholic, stated. The idea of his drinking was so unacceptable that he projected his behavior onto someone else. When I went on vacation, one of my clients dreamt that I was crying and tearful because I couldn't see her that summer. She was projecting her feelings onto me.

Serial Dreams

Often dreams consist of a series of pictures or scenes. Somehow you know they are all connected or part of the same dream, even though each scene is different from the other. These "serial dreams" make sense when you put connecting words between one scene and another. If you think two parts of a dream are related, there is usually a connection between the different scenes. Sometimes different time frames are conveyed in each one. Scene 1 could be a picture of your current situation, Scene 2 could represent the origin of the situation, and Scene 3 could portray a likely future. For example, the first scene could depict the dreamer being distrustful of the present women in his life, the next scene could be like a flashback in a movie where he recalls how his mother abandoned him when he was a child, and the last scene could be of an unhappy old man alienated from his wife and daughters in later years.

A causal connection can also exist between the scenes: the action in one scene could cause the action in the next scene. For instance, the first scene could show the dreamer acting in an arrogant fashion and the next scene could depict her loneliness, the connection between them being that the dreamer's arrogance could lead to being alone in the future. Since dreaming is a picture language, causal and temporal sequences are also portrayed visually.

Sometimes, all three scenes could be different aspects of the same situation. A woman debating whether to marry her boyfriend had three seemingly unconnected dreams but she knew they were all part of the same dream. The first image was of her ex-husband, who was a philanderer; the second was of some very chauvinistic men; and the third was of an annoying, whiny child. The three scenes showed her three aspects of her current boyfriend—his womanizing, his chauvinistic attitude, and his childishness.

All of these mechanisms are ways that dreams communicate certain thoughts and feelings to your awareness. The dream's unique language hints, suggests, plays, and laughs, all to cajole you into awareness. It teases you with its indirectness, allowing you to hear its message when you're ready, much like a wise parent or teacher.

Dream Wisdom

Dreams speak the language of wise men, the language of sages and philosophers. They speak in metaphors, hinting at universal truths. A dream grasps the essence of a situation and presents it to you, sometimes simply and clearly, but frequently in disguised form so that you can choose to look at it and act on it, or to ignore it. Dreams seem to draw upon higher wisdom yet offer daily messages of guidance.

> *The dream is wise*
> *It sees with clear eyes*
> *It never lies*
> *It takes me by surprise*
> *As it answers the why's*
> *Oft-times in disguise*
> *When I arise.*

Summary and Review

Dream interpretation is translating a dream message from one level of consciousness to another, from dream language to everyday language. Dream language is a visual language, using concrete pictures, images, and scenes to depict complex thoughts and ideas. We don't dream in the abstract—we *experience* feelings. Symbols are the vocabulary of this language.

Symbols share common traits with the objects they refer to. These are the key to understanding a symbol's meaning. The meaning of any symbol is unique to the dreamer. Both objects and actions are symbolic in dreams. Since everything in a dream is symbolic, it is important to carefully look at every detail in a dream. Dream language is also a metaphorical language and uses plays on words. It is a humorous, playful, clever language where the mind becomes creative and inventive when freed of mental restraints. It is also an economical language, condensing several ideas into one. Just as dream language has its own vocabulary in the form of symbols, it also has its own rules of logic. Once you understand the dream mechanisms comprising this logic, the dream becomes coherent. Dream language draws upon your inner wisdom, providing you with messages based on your inner knowledge.

Can you think of examples from your own dreams of images or pictures that stood out for you? Of metaphors? Of humor or playfulness? Of wisdom?

3

Remembering and Incubating Dreams

*Put all that truth down so
you never lose it.*

—James Grady

If you are like most people, you probably don't always remember your dreams when you first wake up. You may have a sense that you dreamt something—a thought or feeling that you wake up with—but as soon as you get out of bed and morning reality hits you, the image dissipates and you don't recall what you dreamt. A dream is like a fleeting thought, gone almost as soon as it occurs.

> *We often forget our dreams so speedily;*
> *if we cannot catch them as they are passing*
> *out the door, we never set eyes on them again.*

—William Hazlitt

Remembering Dreams

Here are some practical suggestions for capturing your dreams before they vanish into thin air. If you don't remember your dreams, you might be tempted to say, "I don't dream." You do. We all dream four to five times a night and spend approximately four to five years of our life in the dream state. We all have dreams, we just don't always remember them. Often the reason is simple—inattention. Once you decide to pay attention to your dreams, you'll be surprised by the number of dreams you will recall. It's not necessary to recall *every* dream; one or two a week is plenty to give you food for thought. A potent dream will stay with you, giving you time to look it over and think it through, to study its message and what it's trying to tell you.

Keep a pen and pad of paper by your bedside to record your dreams. The pad gives you a readily available place to write down your dream when you awaken. By the time you get out of bed and hunt for a notebook, the dream will be gone. I suggest having a dream notebook to record your dreams in. Bookstores sell some beautiful journals, and buying one will represent a commitment to honor your dreams. In a sense, you are starting a relationship with your dream life, and like any relationship, the more energy you invest in it, the greater the rewards.

Once you awaken, close your eyes and try to get back into the dream state. Think backwards, "Let's see ... Where was I? ... Oh, yes ... something about a picnic ... John was there ... also Luann ... we were having an argument ..." Try to reconstruct the dream in your mind.

> *I should have lost many a good hit,*
> *had I not set down at once things*
> *that occurred to me in my dreams.*
>
> —Sir Walter Scott

Write down your dream before doing anything else. Don't think that if you rehearse it in your head you will remember it later. You won't! I have frequently had a dream in the middle of the night or early morning but was too lazy to write it down. I would go over it in my head, trying to commit it to memory, but it would be gone by the time I got around to writing it down.

> *You might as well hunt half a*
> *day for a forgotten dream.*
>
> —William Wordsworth

Even if you only recall a small fragment of a dream, write it down anyway. That snippet may be the whole dream. You'll be surprised how much information can be communicated by a single image. Don't dismiss a fragment as unimportant— "Oh, I was only brushing my hair; it couldn't be significant"— write it down, no matter how mundane it may seem.

Following these simple suggestions should help you improve your recollection of your dreams. Remember, one or two dreams a week will give you plenty to think about. If you remember your dreams every night, so much the better; but don't feel compelled to do so. If you currently don't recall any dreams, one or two a week is a good goal. If you follow these instructions and still do not remember your dreams, you may have some fears and attitudes that are getting in the way.

Interference

Here are some attitudes that can interfere with remembering your dreams. See if any of these relate to you.

You Can't Find the Time

"I'm too busy. I don't have time for one more thing. I'm already stressed out. And besides, I need my sleep. It's just too much trouble." Does this sound familiar? In your busy life, you might not feel you have the time or energy to take on one more self-improvement task.

It may seem surprising, but recording your dreams can actually *save* you time and energy, because the time you spend working on your dreams can reduce your stress. So, instead of wasting precious time and energy on vague anxieties and worries, you can uncover the roots of your anxiety by listening to your dreams; you can get clarity on the situation, and the inner peace that comes with it.

You don't have to make recording your dreams a lifetime occupation. Just writing down one dream a week may be enough. You don't need to interrupt your sleep. You can simply write down the first dream you remember when you awake. However, if a dream is important enough that it wakes you up, write it down and try to uncover its message. Doing so could save you many sleepless nights later on.

You're Trying Too Hard

You may not remember your dreams because you may simply be working too hard at it. If you keep a dream notebook by your bedside and consciously suggest to yourself night after night to remember your dream, but you still have little success, maybe you can ease up for a while. You may be trying too hard. Like when we tell ourselves we *must* get some sleep, we usually just get more tense. Tell yourself that when you are ready, you will remember a dream.

You're Afraid of What You'll Find

You May be Hesitant to Hear What Your Dreams Have to Tell You.

Laura couldn't remember any dreams for over two years. She was in an unhappy marriage and tried to distract herself from thinking about it by keeping busy. She was consciously afraid that if she had a dream about her marriage as it really was, she would have to get a divorce.

Being aware of a problem doesn't mean we have to act on it. It just means we have some clarity about why we feel the way we do. We can make choices about what to do with this information. If you dream about the troubles at work, it doesn't mean you have to quit your job; if you become aware of your anger, it doesn't mean you have to divorce your spouse. People who have lost loved ones sometimes don't recall their dreams for fear the dreams would evoke feelings that are too painful. If this is the case with you, just trust that you will remember your dreams when you are ready to deal with these feelings.

You Think Dreams Are Meaningless

A more common reason why some people don't remember their dreams is the attitude that dreams don't mean anything. These people will say, "Why should I pay attention to my dreams? Dreams are not important" or "I don't believe in dreams, anyway." You probably wouldn't have gotten this far in the book if you felt this way, but to people who state that dreams are meaningless, I sometimes ask them how much they know about dreams, how much they have read about them, what research they have studied, and so on. They usually admit that they are only expressing their opinion. Often their statements are made dogmatically without any knowledge of the research that has been done on dreams.

Although there is not as much research on dreams as there is in other areas of psychology due to the difficulty of studying them in the laboratory, most findings suggest that dreams are far from meaningless: dreams reflect your personality and your everyday life (Hall 1953, Hall and Dornhoff 1963, Winget et al. 1972, Koch-Sheras 1985). In controlled experiments, events that were "planted" the day before, such as watching a violent film or being in an emotionally charged therapy session, surfaced in the subject's dreams. Studies also show that individuals can control their dreaming through pre-sleep instructions. Later on in this chapter, I will discuss how you can learn to suggest to yourself to dream on specific topics. Dreams are not random events: people dream about what concerns them. In my first book on dreams, I reviewed the research findings in detail. It is not my intention to repeat that process here except to assure you that quite a bit of research literature indicates dreams are significant and not just meaningless pictures we have in our minds.

In a seminar I was teaching, one of my students rejected the importance of dreams because they could not be observed or measured directly. I suggested she incubate a dream about her resistance to dreams. Because of her curiosity and open-mindedness, she was willing to give it a try. That night she dreamt she was exploring an underground cave. In the dream, she was afraid. As a result of this dream, she was able to face some of her fears about going "underground" and exploring another level of awareness. She had to *experience* the dream for herself before she could pronounce dreams meaningful. As always, experience is the best teacher. Now, years later, she often talks about how her dreams relate to her present situations.

> *The true art of memory is the art of attention.*
>
> —Samuel Johnson

The most important element in recalling our dreams is the amount of work we put into it. The relationship between you and your dreams works both ways: you will get out of them what you are willing to give to them. To develop a powerful relationship with your dreams, you must nurture them in the same way you would nurture a new friendship: giving time, attention, and respect. This means making a solid commitment. Most people find that when they make a conscious effort to spend fifteen minutes every morning writing *something* in their dream journal—whether they remembered their dreams or not—they started to recall their dreams. Those fifteen minutes are about the best investment you can make to your inner life.

Incubating Dreams

When you need some guidance on a specific decision or problem, you can actually turn to your dreams for advice, just as you would to a trusted friend. Have you ever slept on a problem and come up with a solution? That's dream incubation. You go over a situation in your mind and ask your dreams to give you an answer. Just as a hen sits on its eggs till they hatch, you can sleep on a problem and let a solution develop. As I discussed in chapter 1, the incubation stage is essential to the creative process. Dreaming offers a free-flowing state of mind where connections are easily made, where you can remove the blocks that hinder your creativity.

The net of the sleeper catches fish.

—Greek proverb

It may sound like magic, but it isn't. Your dreams often focus on your last waking thoughts. In dream incubation, you try to make certain that the problem you want to dream about is the last thing on your mind before you fall asleep.

Here are some well-proven suggestions on incubating a dream. Experts have come up with some steps to focus on your last waking thoughts so that you might dream about them.

Before you go to sleep, write down a discussion of the problem you want guidance on. For example, you can jot down the pros and cons of staying in a specific job situation. You can write down all of your observations and feelings about a particular person you're not getting along with. Or you could write down some thoughts about a project you are working on where you are feeling stuck. You could write a page or so about the situation.

Writing down your thoughts and feelings serves as a mental preparation, laying the groundwork for these ideas to solidify and take shape in a dream. It's like taking notes before starting to write an essay: it gets the ideas down. Writing is not always necessary—much of the preparation is mental and goes on in our heads. However, putting it down on paper can help you clarify your ideas.

Find a phrase that summarizes the problem you want to sleep on and repeat it to yourself over and over before going to sleep. You could, for example, ask, "Should I stay in this job or not?" or "What should I do about my relationship with Mary?" or "What is blocking me from working on this project?" You can ask for a dream about any area in your life that you would like help on.

Write down the dream immediately after you wake up. Don't judge it. Don't say, "I asked for a dream about getting married, and I'm dreaming about buying a car." The connection may be clear later on. In the meantime, just write it down! Mark and Laura had been living together for several years and had a very good relationship. However, every time that Laura brought up the subject of marriage, Mark would respond that it wasn't necessary, "a marriage license is only a piece of paper." He could not see any advantages to getting that piece of paper. I asked him to have a dream about his feelings concerning commitment. Here's what he said in our next meeting:

> I dreamt I bought a car but hadn't signed the papers yet. I was driving it but wasn't sure if it was really mine or not, like they could take it back at any minute. I wondered who was responsible for it and if I would be held liable without having signed the papers yet.

After writing down the dream, Mark saw the connection between buying a car and getting married, and the importance of that "piece of paper."

It is interesting to note that similar instructions have been used in traditional bedtime rituals to receive dream answers. The Jewish dream ritual, *she'elat chalom* (literally, "dream question") sometimes consisted of writing the question on a parchment, putting it under one's head, and asking for a dream to answer the question. It contains similar elements to modern dream incubation techniques: a relaxed state where the mind is receptive to creative input, a great deal of repetition, and a commitment to remember the dream, record it, and understand its message.

When I talk about dream incubation, I usually caution and say that this is not magic, that you can only get solutions that you already *know* at some level. For example, you cannot ask, "What are the numbers to this week's winning lottery ticket?" Dream incubation is not the lazy way out. It's not like saying, "Oh, I don't have to think about it; I'll let my dream tell me." You still have to do the groundwork—thinking about and analyzing your problem. Only then can you give yourself room to sleep on it and allow its solution to incubate in your mind. In that sense, the dreams are not very different from most good ideas that come after lots of hard work. When you let go for a while and allow your mind to relax and your ideas to percolate, you can often come up with the answers.

Lottie was procrastinating about writing her thesis—so much so that she didn't even look up the relevant research literature on her topic. She didn't do any of the groundwork. She just hoped that somehow through osmosis, she would get the whole thesis written in her sleep. She asked her dreams for guidance. That night, she dreamt she was in a library collecting books on her topic. The message was clear-cut: "If you want help, you need to go to the library and do your research." Dream incubation is not a shortcut to solutions; it doesn't mean abandoning all the hard, conscious reasoning and analysis that we give to a problem. It just adds another dimension to the search, using *all* of the resources open to us. By involving the right brain as well as the left brain, we use *all* of our knowledge and wisdom.

Summary and Review

Dreams are fleeting and vanish into thin air unless you have a net with which to catch them. *To recall your dreams,* keep a journal and a pen by the bed to remind you to have dreams and to record them. Once you awaken, close your eyes and try to get back into the dream state. Write down your dreams *as soon as you wake up.* Don't judge them. Even a small fragment can be significant. You don't need to remember all of your dreams—

one or two a week is enough. *To incubate a dream*, have a discussion with yourself—preferably on paper—regarding the problem you want to dream about. Select a specific phrase that summarizes your question and repeat it over and over before going to sleep. Write down the dream immediately after waking.

Here are some *attitudes that interfere with dream recall*. If you have difficulty remembering your dreams, ask yourself if any of these may describe your situation.

- "I'm too busy."
- "I don't have time."
- "I'm already stressed out."
- "I need my sleep."
- "It's too much trouble."
- "I *must* have a dream."
- "I don't want to know what's going on because I'll have to deal with it."
- "I'm afraid my dreams will be too painful."
- "Dreams are not important."

Remember, dreams are like relationships: the more you put into them, the more you get out of them!

Part 2

Interpreting Your Dreams

4

The Interpretive Process: An Overview

A dream is a translation of waking life.

—René Magritte

So how do you go about translating a dream back into every-day language? As you saw in chapter 2, dream interpretation is a translation from one level of awareness to another, from the obvious dream story to its underlying meaning. To translate dream language into everyday language, you need to find the common denominator of the dream and its waking counterpart. The common denominator serves as the bridge or link between the dream symbols and what they stand for. The following diagram illustrates this relationship:

Dream language	*Common denominator*	**Everyday language**
	(Bridge) ⟶	

This common denominator is usually a trait that is shared by both the symbol and the object it refers to. For example, in a dream, a dog could represent a loyal husband because they both share the common trait of loyalty. *To interpret a dream we must find the common features shared by the two levels of consciousness so that we can translate the dream story into its original form.* The following diagram makes this clear:

Symbol	*Common features* ⟶	**Meaning**
Dog	*Loyal* ⟶	**Husband**

Interpreting a dream is very much like doing a jigsaw puzzle: there is no single way to do it. You have to start somewhere, and every piece you fit together makes it easier to make the next piece fit, until all the pieces are connected. This is how you do dream analysis, slowly and patiently, piece by piece, until you see the whole picture. Sometimes you can't find all the pieces, and you have an incomplete puzzle. That is okay. Even if you can only interpret part of a dream, you get something. You might still find the missing pieces the next day, or even in a later dream. An incomplete interpretation is always better than an incorrect interpretation.

Interpreting a Dream

Dreams are the true interpretations
of our inclinations, but art is required
to sort and understand them.

—Montaigne

The ideal situation for analyzing a dream is with the help of another person, usually a therapist, to ask the questions and trigger the associations. This process allows for a clear distinction between the analytical side of the dialogue (which stays on track and asks the questions) and the intuitive side (which makes the metaphorical connections).

We can also learn to perform this question-and-answer process by ourselves. What follows are a series of steps you can do on your own that will make the process of dream interpretation easier. Included are a number of questions you can ask yourself that can help clarify the meaning of a dream. I have found in my own experience that this process works best when I am in that receptive state of mind directly upon awakening, when I am still operating in a state of consciousness where I am open to new ideas and make connections easily, when my right brain is in full swing. The left brain is necessary to ask the questions and to keep me on track, but I don't want it to interrupt the free-flowing state of the right.

When doing the interpretive process alone, write down your dream, because you may forget important details later on. This will free up your mind for the interpretive work; writing the dream in full allows your right brain to come up with the associations spontaneously since your left brain doesn't have to work at remembering the details. This means you don't have to constantly shift between your analytical and intuitive modes of thinking.

In order to illustrate the step-by-step interpretation process, I will use a dream I have had many years ago:

> I am taking my colleagues to lunch in a restaurant. I look at my salad plate and realize that there is a comb in my salad. I am somewhat embarrassed as it may reflect on me since I brought my co-workers to this restaurant, and I wonder if I should call attention to it. I decide to confront the server. "There is a comb in my salad," I say. She looks very unconcerned and nonchalant and doesn't take the complaint seriously. I decide this is unacceptable service and that I will never frequent that restaurant again.

Before going through the basic steps, it is usually best to try to figure out what the dream is about.

- Do I have any idea what the dream is about?

Sometimes you already know the meaning of the dream and have a notion what the different symbols refer to. In the case of an obvious dream, we can skip some of the steps later on. In the case of my restaurant dream, I simply had no idea.

Summarize the Dreamer's Actions

The first step in dream interpretation is to summarize your actions in the dream in a couple of sentences.

- What were you doing in the dream?

- What were you feeling?

This step focuses not only on your actions in the dream, but also on your thoughts and feelings. You are trying to get the general theme or plot of the dream. Just as in a puzzle, it is usually easiest to start with a frame and then fill it in with the missing pieces.

- Describe the dream in the third person, as though it were a story.

- What is the plot or story line?

- Try to put the plot into one or two sentences.

It can be helpful to describe the dream in the third person as a story happening to someone else. Why only a sentence or two? If you try to capture the entire dream, you might get bogged down describing everything you did in minute detail, thereby missing the forest for the trees. Why the third person? This way you get some distance between yourself and the dream, which helps you see it more objectively. For example:

> This is a story about a woman who takes her colleagues out for lunch, is embarrassed by the poor service she is getting, complains but is met by nonchalance, so she decides never to go to the restaurant again.

When telling the dream story, it's helpful to stay away from the nouns—the objects and symbols—and focus mainly on the verbs—the actions. You will get to the "comb" and the "server" later on. For the time being, concentrate on the action alone. By focusing on the action, you can summarize this dream even further:

> The dreamer is getting poor service and is met by nonchalance when she complains.

Relate the Actions to Your Waking Life

Once you know what the main action of the dream is, you can try to figure out the relationship between the dream and your waking life.

- Where in my waking life am I experiencing the same feelings as in the dream?

- Are the actions in the dream similar to any situation in my everyday life?

This question links the action in the dream to the action in your waking lives. Where in my life am I getting poor service which embarrasses me in front of my colleagues. Where are my complaints being met by nonchalance? As soon as I asked myself this question, I recalled that the previous day, a colleague had mentioned to me that the answering service which took my calls had acted in a rude manner. When I had called the woman at the service to complain, she had shown the same nonchalant attitude as the woman in the dream. By discovering what part of your waking life the dream refers to, you are able to put the dream in context.

Find the Focal Point

Once you know the context of the dream, you can then define the symbols *within that context*. You have the frame of the puzzle, and now you can begin to fill in the different pieces. As with a jigsaw puzzle, a good starting point is a piece that stands out, the focal point.

The *focal point* is the part of the dream that stands out, is out of context, doesn't fit, or doesn't make sense.

- What stands out for me?

- What is not clear?

- Is there anything that doesn't fit or doesn't make sense?

Which part of the restaurant dream is least understandable? As I looked at the dream, I saw that the comb was clearly out of place. What is a comb doing in a salad? The comb is the focal point.

Some dreams don't have anything particular that stands out. If this is the case, we can go to the next step and define all the symbols in the dream and your own experiences with them.

Define the Symbols

To arrive at the meaning of a symbol, you have to define it. You don't ask, for example, "What is a comb to me?" You ask, "What is a *comb*?" Next you need to uncover your own unique associations to the symbol. You then use the words in the definition and the associations to get at the symbol's meaning.

- What is _____ (symbol)?

- What am I reminded of when I think of the words I used to define _____?

- What have been my own associations and experiences with _____?

- What part has _____ played in my life?

- Is there a part of me that's like _____?

I begin with the focal point of the dream, the comb, defining the symbol and uncovering my own particular associations to it. A comb is something I use on my hair to make me look good. It belongs in the bathroom, not the kitchen. A comb is clearly unacceptable in food. The words used in the definition and the specific associations to the symbol are the common denominator, the link between the symbol and the object it refers to. What was I reminded of when I thought of something unacceptable that made me look bad in front of my colleagues? The comb reminded me of rudeness to my callers, which was unacceptable and made me look bad to my callers.

I went on to define the other symbols in the dream: the *server*—someone who is giving me service but seems nonchalant—reminded me of the woman I had complained to; my *colleagues* represented my colleagues who have to interact with my service; the *restaurant*—a place that offers you service that you often provide for yourself—reminded me of my answering service. In dream analysis, we try to find the common features between the symbols and what they represent. As we define the symbols and give our associations to them, we discover the common denominator of the dream language and the situation it relates to in our waking life. By defining these symbols and their associations, we get the new meaning. The diagram on page 73 shows the relationship between the symbols and the objects they refer to.

Rewrite the Dream Story

Now you can rewrite the dream story, using the new meanings. In this step, you simply substitute the new meanings for the symbols in the dream story as in the diagram on page 74.

Note that the verbs—the dreamer's *actions*—remain the same. Only the nouns—the *symbols* or *objects*—change. The actions are "getting poor service," "being embarrassed," "complaining," "being met by nonchalance," etc. The symbols—the restaurant, the comb, and the server—stand for objects in my

Anatomy of a Dream

Dream language	Common denominator (Bridge)	Everyday language
	──────▶	
Comb salad	*Unacceptable service* ──────▶	Rudeness in to callers
Server	*Person I complain to: nonchalant; unconcerned* ──────▶	Person at answering service
Colleagues	*People I work with; peers* ──────▶	Colleagues
Restaurant	*Place I use to provide service for colleagues; reflects on me* ──────▶	Answering service

- What is it trying to tell me?

- What is the moral of the story?

- Why do I need to remind myself of this now?

The message seems clear: The service I was getting was unacceptable and I should not use it any longer. The dream highlighted this reality and brought it to my attention. I realized that being rude to my colleagues was as unacceptable as having a comb in my food.

Apply the Message to your Waking Life

- How can I apply the message to my waking life?

I decided to switch to another service.

Summary and Review

It is useful to look at every dream as a story about the dreamer. First try to get the main theme or action of the dream and relate it to waking life. Then you can define and associate to every symbol within the context of the dream in order to rewrite a new dream story. Then you can look at the message—what the dream is trying to tell you—and how you can apply that to your waking life. I will elaborate on each of these steps in later chapters and give you a chance to practice them. On the following pages is a summary of the step-by-step procedure to understand your dreams. Use these basic steps and ask yourself these questions when looking at your dreams. I suggest writing your responses down to make the process clearer, and to keep you on track should you tend to get lost.

Steps in Dream Interpretation

Some Things to Think about When Looking at a Dream

Before going through the steps, ask yourself if you can figure out what the dream is about.

- Do I have any idea what the dream is about?

Summarize your actions in the dream in a couple of sentences.

- What were you doing in the dream?

- What were you feeling?

- Describe the dream in the third person as though it were a story.

- What is the plot or story line?

- Try to put the plot into one or two sentences.

Relate your actions to your waking life.

- Where in my waking life am I experiencing the same feelings as in the dream?

- Are the actions in the dream similar to any situation in my everyday life?

Find the focal point.

- What stands out for me?

- What is not clear?

- Is there anything that doesn't fit or doesn't make sense?

Define each symbol in the dream and your own associations to it.

- What is _____ (symbol)?

- What am I reminded of when I think of the words I used to describe _____?

- What are my own associations and experiences with _____?

- What part has _____ played in my life?

- Is there a part of me that is like _____?

Use the words in the definition and associations to the symbol to get at its underlying meaning.

Rewrite the dream story, using the new meanings.

Unlock the dream's message.

- What is the message of the dream?

- What is it trying to tell me?

- What is the moral of the story?

- Why do I need to remind myself of this right now?

Apply the message to your waking life.

- How can I apply this message to my waking life?

A word of caution about the basic steps: This formula is basically a left brain activity, whereas dream interpretation is more of a right brain activity. An interpretation doesn't always fall together as neatly and logically as a mathematical equation. The steps are meant to *guide* and *not to restrict*. You will find that associations are often made outside of the defined steps. These steps are merely guidelines so that you don't get lost or miss the forest for the trees when looking at a dream.

5

Summarizing the Dreamer's Actions

A dream is the theater where the dreamer is at once scene, actor, prompter, stage manager, author, audience and critic.

—Carl Jung

As you have already seen in previous chapters, dream interpretation consists of finding the common denominator that links the dream story and what it refers to. This diagram demonstrates this relationship:

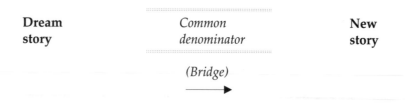

Dream story	*Common denominator*	New story

(Bridge)

→

By far the easiest way to connect the dream to the real world is through the dreamer's behavior. The first step in dream interpretation is therefore to summarize your actions in the dream, so that you will be able to find a matching counterpart in waking life.

Summarize the Dreamer's Action

When you describe a dream, you usually hear a story. It may be long or short, clear or nonsensical, rambling or straightforward, plain or elaborate, but it's a story nevertheless: *Someone does something.* Every story, regardless of content, has a protagonist in it: the dreamer. *Every dream is about the dreamer.*

Even thought you may have dreams about another person, the dream is not about that person but about yourself. You can ask why you are choosing to dream about that particular person. What does that person represent to you? For example, we can ask ourselves, "Why am I dreaming about George Washington? Is there a message in there for me about his behavior?" It is very simplistic to say, "Oh, I just dreamt about him because I saw a show about him on television last night." You have to ask yourself why of all the events of the previous day did you choose to dream about this one. What message might it have for you? So even though the dream may ostensibly be about George Washington, or any other person, you need to look at the dreamer's actions even if all the dreamer is doing is observing someone else's behavior.

To understand a dream, *you need to look at what the dreamer is doing in the dream.* It is easy to get sidetracked by details when you think about a dream, focusing on the objects or characters. If you learn to ignore the content and only focus on the dreamer's behavior, we can get the gist of the story faster. Try to focus only on the dreamer's actions and feelings as you hear the following dream story.

> My wife and I are all ready to go on a hot air balloon ride. We had been planning this trip for a long time and were very excited. We inflate the balloon, and we are all prepared to go. There is a sense of anticipation and excitement in the air. The only thing holding us up is my brother. We are waiting for him to arrive to pilot the balloon so that we can start this adventure. We wait and wait but he never shows up.

What is the dreamer doing in the dream? What is he thinking and feeling? If this were a movie you saw or a story you read, how would you summarize the plot? Take a few minutes to describe this dream in the third person, as though it were a story. Try to summarize the actions in a couple of sentences before going on to the next paragraph.

Here is a two-sentence summary of the dream:

> The dreamer is eagerly anticipating a long planned event with his wife. They are held up by someone who never shows up.

Retelling the dream in the third person puts some distance between yourself and the dream, enabling you to look at it more objectively, as you would look at a story. At first you may have difficulty summarizing a dream, particularly if it was long and rambling. If you dwell on the details, you may get lost in them. If you just came out of a movie, and someone asked what it was about, you wouldn't retell it scene by scene but would summarize the story in a few words: "It was a story about a woman who divorces her husband and how she survives on her own" or "It was a story about a man who cannot make a commitment and the effects it has on his life" or "It was a story about a guy who can't show feelings until others break through the armor." Most stories can be summarized in a few sentences.

Although it's usually easy to spot the central action in the dream, at times it may be difficult to do so. If you're having trouble focusing on the action, try taking out all the nouns in the dream and replacing them with pronouns. If you substitute *someone* or *something* or *somewhere* for all the nouns in the dream, the plot becomes clearer. For example, if you ignored the nouns or symbols in Mark's dream, you would only be left with the action as follows:

> The dreamer is *anticipating* something with someone and is *kept waiting* by someone who never gets there.

Some dreams are like surrealistic movies where if someone asked you what the plot was, you couldn't really articulate it. Even then, however, you can start by trying to recapture the general mood. For example, "It was a very negative film" or "I'm not sure what it was about but the general feeling was of nostalgia" or "The whole dream had an eerie quality to it." In a dream, you might have a vague feeling of chaos or of turmoil, of sadness or of dread. Try to put those feelings and sensations into words. Then you can look for a relationship between the feelings in the dream and those in your waking life.

> *It is in our idleness, in our dreams, that the submerged truth sometimes comes to the top.*
>
> —Virginia Woolf

Relating the Dream Action to Real Life

Once you have a simple summary of the dreamer's actions in the dream, you can look for a matching counterpart in waking life. Remember my dream with the comb in the salad? I needed to ask a few questions to narrow down which part of my life the dream was referring to.

- Where in my life am I getting poor service?

- Where in my life am I complaining and getting no response?

- Where in my life am I feeling embarrassed in front of my colleagues?

- Where in my waking life am I experiencing the same actions and feelings as in the dream?

Most of the time asking the question, "Where in my life am I . . ." gives us a clue to the roots of the dream story. The diagram shows this connection:

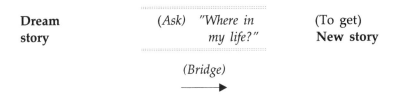

When we know the real life roots of the dream story, we can rewrite it with its original meaning. Remember the "hot air balloon" and the man waiting for his brother? Mark, the dreamer, asked himself, "Where in my waking life am I anticipating a long planned event with my wife but am held back?"

He immediately saw the similarities between the actions in the dream and the actions in his waking life: he and his wife had been talking for a long time about having a baby but he would get cold feet whenever they would come close to making this happy event a reality. As he associated to the dream, he recognized that his brother represented the part of him that was afraid of growing up, and that this fear had its origins in unresolved childhood conflicts with his brother. He could then rewrite the dream story as follows:

> I am eager to have a child but my fear of growing up which stems from unresolved childhood conflicts with my brother is holding me back.

Sometimes the real-life counterpart of your dream is not so clear. Do not despair! You can still get clues from the setting or the characters in the dream. For example, if the dream takes place in your childhood home, it most likely refers to the childhood origins of your current problems. If the characters are family members, it probably refers to your family; if the characters are people you work with, it may have to do with work. The symbols themselves can also provide the common bridge. What am I reminded of when I think of _____ ? What am I reminded of when I think of someone who is nonchalant when I complain? What am I reminded of when I think of being frustrated trying to reach a goal? The questions "Where in my life?" and "What am I reminded of?" can bring on the "aha" experience, that exciting moment when you recognize the connection between the dream features and the everyday features they refer to.

> *Why does the eye see a thing more clearly*
> *in dreams than the imagination when awake?*
>
> —Leonardo da Vinci

Dream Practice

The rest of the chapter will give you an opportunity to practice the first step in dream interpretation: summarizing the dreamer's actions in a couple of sentences. The following are all actual dreams told to me by clients. As you read these dreams, pay attention to the dreamer's behavior.

- What is the dreamer doing?
- What is the dreamer thinking and feeling?
- Describe the dream as though it were a story in the third person.
- What is the plot or story line?
- Try to summarize the actions in a sentence or two.

For this exercise to be most helpful, place a piece of paper over the summary following each dream and write down your answer before reading the summary. Don't worry if your own words are somewhat different from the ones I have used. The goal is simply to get to the heart of the dream.

> I discover some relatives from a foreign land and talk to them. They start to tell me about their religious beliefs. They say they don't eat sugar and believe that it is evil. They have blinders on their eyes to keep them from making eye contact with each other, because they think that is bad. I think their beliefs are strange and absurd but I doubt myself and don't say anything. We are of the same faith, and I wonder if I'm wrong in my beliefs.

The dreamer meets people whose beliefs he thinks are absurd. Instead of challenging these people, he questions his own beliefs.

> All night long I kept having dreams that I wanted to sing, and I was looking all over for a room where I could sing but I just couldn't find a room.

The dreamer wants to do something and looks all over for a place to do it but can't find it.

> I am floating in a raft. It is very shaky. I have a few belongings, and I'm trying to hold them all together. My umbrella falls off, and I jump down to retrieve it. Then I'm afraid I'm going to drown. I am terrified but I finally make it up without drowning.

The dreamer is in a precarious and unstable situation and nearly drowns trying to hold it all together.

> I'm in a doctor's office, and I'm going to have a baby. The doctor, who is a family practice doctor, is going through everything and doing a good job, showing me slides and ultrasound pictures and quoting statistics. I realize that I am very concerned about the childbirth and need to tell him of my apprehensions, what I want done, and so on. I tell him that I want to discuss my concerns with him, that I had talked to Dr. X, my previous gynecologist, and that it had really helped. The doctor agreed it was important but brushed me off, like we'd get back to that later, at another time. I was disappointed and frustrated because childbirth was my most important concern and I wanted to be as prepared as possible for it but we never got around to that.

The dreamer doesn't get a chance to discuss what is most important to her. Her concerns get brushed off, and she feels disappointed and frustrated.

> I am flying in this dream, and it's a good feeling but I'm afraid I might fall to the ground and crash. I

experiment letting go and I fall and fall and then I make myself go up again, and then I fall faster and faster, and I'm afraid to look down but I fall to the ground, and there's a shock absorber on the ground, and I bounce back and nothing happens to me, and I start flying again.

The dreamer is afraid he will fall and crash, but when he does, he bounces back.

I am in a race. I jump in late but I end up in second place anyway, even though I started later than the others. I am wearing my Colorado State T-shirt, and I take it off because it is weighing me down. I then go on with the race.

The dreamer starts out late but catches up and does pretty well. She removes something that is weighing her down.

I was in my old hometown, and it was a nightmare. There were knives being thrown all over the house. I was terrified, and I left the house. I vowed never to go back again, but I took two jars of raspberry jam with me.

The dreamer survives a terrible situation and ends up taking something good out of it.

I am looking at two apartments: one is empty and has no furniture in it, the other is fully furnished but much too cluttered. The furniture is not up to my taste; it looks very garish, but I feel that at least it's furnished and ready, and it would be easier to move there rather than move to the empty apartment. I wake up, not knowing what to choose.

The dreamer is trying to make a decision. Neither choice is appealing. One is more convenient but not up to her taste.

> I am back in college, and I feel very overwhelmed. I am enrolled in courses I didn't know I was in, and then I find out that I have some tests to take. I am behind in everything, and I am taking this test which I didn't even know I had to take. The instructor passes out the examination sheets, and by mistake gives me the answer sheet. I am tempted to just write down the answers, but I am too honest and give it back and continue taking the test.

The dreamer is unprepared, feels behind, has an opportunity to take the easy way out, but decides not to.

> I am sitting on a porch railing outside my house, and a man comes selling all kinds of junk, all kinds of gimmicky stuff. I buy some of that stuff even though I don't need it. I guess I bought it because he wanted to sell it.

The dreamer does things she doesn't want to do because someone else wants her to.

> I am in a bowling alley with my friends, and Mick asks me to bowl, and I am just not up to it, and he keeps insisting and insisting until I finally throw the ball, and it is a terrible shot. I get angry and walk off and say, "I am just not ready. I told you I didn't want to bowl."

The dreamer does something she doesn't want to do and is not ready for and is angry about it.

> I am driving in my car, going up 48th Street. The brakes don't seem to be working. I try to stop at a stop sign but the car just slows down and I coast and cross the street. There is a woman with me in the car. I am worried about what she thinks of me, and I'm

surprised that she is unconcerned and that nothing happened.

The dreamer cannot seem to slow down. She is worried about how she is seen by others, and surprised by their lack of concern.

I'm a nurse in a hospital, and I am supposed to be taking care of this patient. He is an old man, and I realize that it is time for him to have a bowel movement. I really don't want to have to clean up his excrement. I see an orderly or nurse or something, and I ask that person to take care of my patient. I feel so relieved that I don't have to clean up after him.

The dreamer doesn't want to do something unpleasant. She asks others to do it and feels relieved.

I dreamt that I had stickpins on my tongue. They were very annoying. Every time I'd take them out, they would come back again. This happened every time I moved toward my car. It happened three times. I remember thinking maybe if I don't keep coming back, I'd get rid of them once and for all.

The dreamer gets rid of something annoying but it keeps coming back.

I am looking for a house. It is Number 230. I have the address in my hand but I keep getting lost and can't find it. Someone tries to help me, but when I look for the slip of paper, I can't find it. I lose the slip of paper on which I had written the address and never find it. I never get there.

The dreamer feels lost and can't find what she is looking for.

Jill is telling me a story about Joan Crawford. Apparently she used to torture her husband by following

> him wherever he went. She would make him very jealous by flirting with others. Once she went with him on a cruise and spent the time flirting with someone else.

The dreamer is hearing a story about a woman who tortured her husband and made him jealous. Remember, *the focus is always on the dreamer*. This is a story about the dreamer, not about Joan Crawford.

> I'm talking to Connie, counseling her or something. She wants to work full-time when she retires and also to go to night school. I point out to her that she can't do both—work full-time and go to school. I tell her she needs to cut down and cut out one or the other. Jessica is there too and tells her the same thing, but I think that Connie doesn't want to hear it.

The dreamer is counseling someone and advising her to cut down. The other person doesn't want to hear it.

If you want further practice in summarizing the actions, think of some movies you have seen or books you have read and summarize the protagonist's actions in a couple of sentences.

Summary and Review

Every dream, regardless of content, tells a story about the dreamer. To understand a dream, you need to look at what the dreamer is doing in the dream. The first step in dream interpretation is to summarize the dreamer's actions in the dream. Then you can relate these actions to waking life. In order to get the central action in the dream, describe it in the third person, as though it were a story happening to someone else. Try to summarize the main action in a couple of sentences, ignoring the content and focusing only on the dreamer's actions and feelings. Once you have the plot or story line, you can then ask where in your waking life you experience the same feelings. This will lead you to the new dream story.

Summarize the dreamer's actions in a couple of sentences.

- What were you doing in the dream?

- What were you feeling?

- Describe the dream in the third person, as though it were a story.

- What is the plot or story line?

- Try to put the plot into one or two sentences.

Relate the action to your waking life.

- Where in my waking life am I experiencing the same feelings as in the dream?

- Are the actions in the dream similar to any situation in my everyday life?

To give you some practice working on your own dreams, write down a recent dream, the more recent the better. It is much easier to answer the question "Where in my life am I . . . ?" when you are working with a recent dream. After writing down the dream, rewrite it in the third person as though it were a story happening to someone else. What is the plot or story line? Try to summarize the actions in a couple of sentences. Then try to see if there is a relationship between the dream and your waking life. Ask yourself where in your waking life you are experiencing the same feelings and actions as in the dream.

6

Finding
the Focal Point

The devil is in the details.

—Anonymous
(German proverb)

Once you have summarized the actions of the dream story and related them to your waking life, you can then begin to look at the different symbols in the story. There are usually so many details in a dream that you may not have any idea which one to explore first. In interpreting a dream, you can start with any symbol and then go on to connect the other symbols until you complete the puzzle. Although you can begin with any of the symbols, it is best to start with the *focal point*. Therefore the next step of dream interpretation is finding a focal point, a point of reference from which to begin asking questions.

The Focal Point

Think of the focal point of a dream as you would think of a focal point in a painting. Where is the eye immediately drawn? What catches your attention? What stands out? What is most unusual? What is highlighted? The focal point in a dream is usually that detail that is clearly out of place or difficult to explain. What is a comb doing in my salad? The comb clearly is the focal point of the dream; it's an unusual detail and is not immediately understandable. If you start out with the part of the dream that is most odd, interesting, or out of context, it usually provides an important clue to the meaning of the dream. Everything else in the dream is internally consistent, but a comb in a salad is out of context, and this is what makes it stand out.

> 'Tis strange—but true; for truth
> is always stranger than fiction.
>
> —Lord Byron

Every detail in a dream is there for a reason—*otherwise you would not dream it*. Rather than ignore a striking or inexplicable detail ("oh, that doesn't fit") or try to correct it ("it doesn't make sense so I'll make it fit"), you need to realize that it is *precisely because it doesn't fit* that it is important.

Sometimes the focal point is obvious and can be recognized right away; other times, it's not so easy to spot. In those cases, you can jump to the next step and start defining the different symbols. Sometimes a dream has several strange elements or focal points. In this case, you can start with the detail that stands out the most. At times the focal point could be an emotion rather than an object. It could even be something that just seems important, a detail that holds your interest to the exclusion of other details.

> *An exaggeration is a truth that has lost its temper.*
>
> —Kahlil Gibran

At times, the focal point may be what is missing, as in the example given earlier in the book, of the woman who dreamt of a marriage bed that was missing a leg. You may be tempted to correct a dream by filling in the missing pieces and making it correspond to everyday reality. However, *it is precisely what is strange, odd, out of place, or unexplained that you need to focus on.*

Dream Practice

Look at the following dreams and find a focal point in each. As you review each dream, try to first summarize the dreamer's actions in a couple of sentences and then find the focal point. In looking for a focal point, ask yourself the following questions:

- What stands out here?

- What is not clear?

- Is there anything that doesn't fit or doesn't make sense?

As in the preceding chapter, place a piece of paper over the comments following each dream and write down your answer before reading them. Then go on to the next dream. You will recognize some dreams from the last chapter.

> My father and I are flying from one place to another in an airplane, and we have a layover somewhere. We're looking for a restaurant, and I see "Love's Bar-B-Que" across the highway. I want very much to go there with my dad but he doesn't want to, so we don't go. I felt very disappointed, and I don't remember what happened next.

The dreamer wants to go somewhere with her father but he doesn't want to go, and she feels disappointed. The focal point here is "Love's Bar-B-Que." This detail provided the meaning of the dream for the dreamer, who was always trying to get love from her father and being disappointed when he didn't give it to her.

> There is a big party for me. I remember lots of people from my past were there, including my dead girl-friend and aunt. There is a man at the party who has a contract out on my life. He tells me that it is being done by poison, which is in the hot chocolate, and that I'd drink it at the end of the party. I know I'm going to die but I passively go along with it and don't do anything about it. I try to tell others about it and go whisper to everyone so he won't hear me, "It's in the chocolate!" but I still don't do anything about it. At the end, he says that he just can't do that to me, that I don't deserve to be killed, that I'm too nice and everyone loves me, and he tears up the contract.

The dreamer knows she is to die but doesn't do anything about it. At the end, her life is spared because she doesn't deserve to die. The focal point and the clue to the dream's meaning was the chocolate. The dreamer, a compulsive over-eater with low self-esteem, knew that she was killing herself by the volume of sweets she was consuming. The dream recognized this and also that she didn't deserve this fate. Although other unexplained details exist—the dead girlfriend and the aunt—the chocolate is the central detail and the key to the dream.

> I am in a race. I jump in late but I end up in second place anyway, even though I started later than the others. I am wearing my Colorado State T-shirt, and I take it off because it is weighing me down. I then go on with the race.

The dreamer starts out late but catches up and does pretty well. Something is weighing her down which she removes. The focal point here is the Colorado State T-shirt, which gave a clue to the dream's meaning. In this case, the dreamer went to school at Colorado State and learned some attitudes that interfered with her sexual and social growth. Again, the fact that this detail is mentioned means we should pay attention to it. Why Colorado State of all places? Why didn't she just dream of a T-shirt? The devil is in the details!

> I was in my old hometown, and it was a nightmare. There were knives being thrown all over the house. I was terrified, and I left the house. I vowed never to go back again, but I took two jars of raspberry jam with me.

The dreamer survives a terrible situation and ends up taking something good out of it. The focal point is the raspberry jam, which is clearly out of context. Raspberry jam was the dreamer's favorite, and something she relished very much. Although she had a violent and traumatic childhood, she also has sweet memories of it.

> I am looking at two apartments: one is empty and has no furniture in it, the other is fully furnished but much too cluttered. The furniture is not up to my

> taste; it looks very garish, but I feel that at least it's furnished and ready, and it would be easier to move there than move to the empty apartment. I wake up, not knowing what to choose.

The dreamer is trying to make a decision between something convenient and something that fits her taste. Neither choice is appealing. Although nothing was strange or out of place in this dream, when the dreamer asked herself what stood out for her, she was struck by how garish the furniture was and chose that as the focal point. The dreamer, a single woman who lived by herself and longed to have someone to share her life with, had been dating a man for several months who wanted her to move in with him. She was tempted to do so because then she wouldn't have to be alone. It would also be financially convenient. However, the dream alerted her how "garish" she found him. Although it would be convenient, he was not up to her standards.

> I dreamt that I had stickpins on my tongue. They were very annoying. Every time I'd take them out, they would come back again. This happened every time I moved toward my car. It happened three times. I remember thinking maybe if I don't keep coming back, I'd get rid of them once and for all.

The dreamer gets rid of something annoying but it keeps coming back. The stickpins are an unusual detail and can serve as the focal point. This was one of a series of dreams a woman had while trying to quit her job. She defined and associated to stickpins as "something I use at work," "a sticky situation," "a nuisance; it can prick but not really hurt." Stickpins represented the sticky unpleasantness she associated with her work. Every time she thought that the problems were resolved, they would reappear. Several times she had resolved to quit, only to change her mind. The dream confirmed for her that the relief from the job nuisances was only temporary and that they would only cease if she left her current position. This dream spurred her to eventually resign from her job and not be fooled by temporary respites.

> I am looking for a house. It is Number 230. I have the address in my hand but I keep getting lost and can't find it. Someone tries to help me, but when I look for the slip of paper, I can't find it. I lose the slip of paper on which I had written the address and never find it. I never get there.

The dreamer feels lost and can't find what she's looking for. The detail that is highlighted is "Number 230." The dream goes to a lot of trouble to display this detail, and it is a good idea to start with that number as the focal point. The number gave the clue to the dream. The dreamer had seen a house she liked, which was selling for *230 thousand dollars*, and she didn't know where she would find the money to buy it.

> Jill is telling me a story about Joan Crawford. Apparently, she used to torture her husband by following him wherever he went. She would make him very jealous by flirting with others. Once she went with him on a cruise and spent the time flirting with someone else.

The dreamer listens to a story about a woman who tortured her husband and made him jealous. The focal point in the dream is Joan Crawford. She is clearly highlighted in the dream. The meaning she has for the dreamer is not explained. Why did the dreamer choose this particular symbol? For this dreamer, Joan Crawford represented a glamorous woman to all external appearances but whose family life was marked by abuse, discord, and chaos. By choosing this symbol, the dreamer was reminding herself that her own "Joan Crawford" type of behavior—being pleasant to her husband in public but abusive when they were alone—could be undermining her marriage.

> I have a dream that my father is being tested for an illness, and there is a naked little girl outside. My mother is there too. The name of his illness is "Karpelsini."

The dreamer observes her father being tested for an illness. Although there are several details that stand out here, the one that is least understood is "Karpelsini." It can serve as the focal point in the dream. The dreamer had been trying to come to terms with her father, who abused her when she was a little girl. Karpelsini was a spiritual guru she was familiar with. The dream helped her recognize that her father was a sick man; he had a diseased spirit.

> I am in a store, and I am looking all over to find matching pants for John and me for our wedding. I look all over and can't seem to find them.

The dreamer is searching for something in this dream and finds something she wasn't looking for. What stands out here? What doesn't make sense? The first reaction to hearing this dream may be "Since when does a bride wear pants to a wedding?" The matching pants are the focal point in this dream. Frequently we may have a dream with a small detail like this one and make the mistake of dismissing it as insignificant. However, *the detail is there for a reason.* In this case, that detail was the clue to the dream. The dreamer was concerned about who would "wear the pants" in her marriage and was searching for a relationship of equality. She also saw that by looking for an equal relationship, she may have suppressed some of her "feminine" feelings by not wearing a bridal gown.

> I am in a barber shop. I am angry at waiting for the barber to come and cut my hair. There is a young kid

> smoking. I speak up and tell him not to. He stops and
> then starts again. I tell him again to stop.

The dreamer is angry waiting and also speaks up to someone about something he does that bothers her. This dream by a middle-aged woman has an incongruous detail in it that can easily be overlooked as insignificant. Women do not go to barbers. The focal point in the dream is the barber shop. When interpreting this dream, our impulse may be to correct it and say she was at the hairdresser's. However, this detail turned out to be quite important to understanding the dream's meaning. The dreamer was having difficulty accepting her homosexual orientation.

> I had a dream about my grandmother. I was in her
> room, and we were talking about something or other.
> I really don't remember much of the dream, but I
> woke up with an overwhelming feeling of love that I
> can't describe. It was so beautiful, I just want to hold
> on to it. I can still see her. She looked absolutely radi-
> ant, absolutely lovely. I still feel like crying when I
> think of how beautiful she was and how much I love
> her.

The dreamer sees her grandmother and is overwhelmed by love. What stands out here is the overwhelming feeling of love the dreamer has for her grandmother who had recently died.

Some dreams have more than one focal point. A dream can have several unusual details, parts that are unclear, or points that stand out. Other dreams may not have anything that seems surprising, strange, or puzzling. If you cannot find a focal point, you can proceed directly to the next step of dream interpretation: defining the symbols and providing your associations to them.

Summary and Review

Once you get the dream story and relate it to waking life, the next step in understanding your dreams is finding a focal point from which to start asking questions. The focal point is usually that detail that is least understandable. If you start out with the part of the dream that is most unusual, surprising, or out of context, it frequently provides a clue to the meaning of the dream. Although it may be tempting to dismiss or correct parts of the dream that don't make sense, these strange details need to be examined and explained. Every detail is there for a reason—otherwise, you would not dream it.

In order to find the focal point, ask yourself the following questions:

- What stands out for me?

- What is not clear?

- Is there anything that doesn't fit or doesn't make sense?

7

Translating
the Symbols

*A definition is the enclosing a wilderness
of idea within a wall of words.*

—Samuel Butler

After summarizing the actions, relating them to waking life, and finding a focal point, the next step in dream interpretation is to unlock the meaning of each symbol in the dream. Since symbols are unique to the person dreaming them, the only way to know what the different symbols stand for is to define them and pinpoint the dreamer's specific associations to them.

> *The chief merit of language is clarity ...*
> —Galen

Unlocking a Symbol's Meaning

It is worth repeating: *there are no universal symbols*. You cannot go to a dictionary and find out what a symbol means, because different symbols mean different things to different people. Every symbol is unique to the dreamer, and the only way to get at its meaning is through your own definition and associations to it. *The words in the definition and associations can provide the link between the symbol and its underlying meaning*; they are the common denominator shared by the symbol and what it stands for, as the following diagram illustrates:

| **Symbol** | *Common features* *(Definition & Associations)* | **Meaning** |

(Bridge)
⟶

Defining a Symbol

To understand the meaning of a symbol, we have to *define* it. Jane had a dream that she was Barry Goldwater. When asked for a definition, she said, "Goldwater is a politician who speaks his mind." The symbol "Barry Goldwater" represented that part of her that was assertive and spoke up. The following diagram shows this relationship:

Barry Goldwater	*(Definition)* "*someone who speaks his mind*"	Assertive Self

(Bridge)

———▶

Barry Goldwater could represent different things to different people depending on who is defining the symbol. Don't say, "Oh, everyone knows who Barry Goldwater is" or "Everyone knows what a chair is"; define the symbol anyway. The specific words you use to describe the object are a clue to what it represents for you. Don't ask yourself, "What is a chair to me?" Ask, "What is a chair?" Pretend you are defining it for someone who has never seen a chair before. One dream analyst suggests pretending you are defining and describing the object to someone from another planet. What words would you use in your definition? Those words will be a clue to the common denominator between the symbol and what it stands for.

> *We must think things, not words, or at least we must constantly translate our words into the facts for which they stand, if we are to keep to the real and the true.*

> —Oliver Wendell Holmes

Kevin had a dream about the Kennedys. When asked for a definition ("How would I describe the Kennedys to someone from another planet?"), he replied, "A large Catholic family that maintains a strong public image but has had many tragedies." When asked "What are you reminded of when you think of a large Catholic family that maintains a strong public image but has had many tragedies?" Kevin thought of his own

| **Kennedys** | *"a large Catholic family that maintains a strong public image but had has many tragedies"* | **My family** |

(Bridge)
——▶

family and recognized that the Kennedys were a symbol for them, as the diagram shows:

The definition and description include the common features that link the symbol and the object it represents. To find out what a symbol means, define it and see if the words in the definition trigger a meaning. "What am I reminded of when I think of the words I use to describe the symbol? What am I reminded of when I think of someone who speaks his mind? What am I reminded of when I think of a large Catholic family that maintains a strong public image but has had many tragedies?"

Defining Your Associations to a Symbol

After you find your definition, you can ask for your own particular associations to the symbol itself.

These associations are called *to-the-point associations*; they are your direct associations to a particular symbol. To find your to-the-point associations, ask yourself the following questions:

- What am I reminded of when I think of a particular symbol?

- What have been my own associations and experiences with it?

Rewriting the Dream Story

Dream story

*In the **restaurant,** I notice a **comb in my salad.***
*I am embarrassed in front of my **colleagues** as it makes*
me look bad. I wonder whether to call attention to it.
*I confront the **server** and complain. She is nonchalant*
and unconcerned and doesn't take the complaint seriously.
I decide not to give them my business.

Just change the symbols to their new meaning.

New story

*In the **answering service,** I notice **rude behavior.***
*I am embarrassed in front of my **colleagues** as it makes*
me look bad. I wonder whether to call attention to it.
*I confront the **woman at the service** and complain. She is*
nonchalant and unconcerned and doesn't take the complaint
seriously. I decide not to give them my business.

life—my answering service, rudeness to my callers, and the
person I complain to.

Unlock the Dream Message

Once you have the new story, you can find out what the
message of the dream is for you.

- What is the message of the dream?

- What part has that symbol played in my life?

- Is there a part of me that is like that symbol?

For instance, Kevin asked himself, "What are my own associations to the Kennedys? What part have they played in my life? Is there a part of me that is like them?" You associate both to the symbol itself and to the words defining it to get at the symbol's meaning.

> *Language is an inventory of human experience.*
> —L. W. Lockhart

To-the-point associations are different from free associations. To-the-point associations are just that—*to the point.* They ask the question: "What am I reminded of when I think of this specific symbol?" Kevin's to-the-point association to the Kennedys was that he frequently compared them to his own family because they were Catholic and had many children, and this set of associations, together with his definition, immediately led him to make the connection to his own family. Free association, which used to be popular in dream analysis, offers random connections that can detract from a symbol's meanings. Free associations can go something like this: "The Kennedys . . . I read something about them in the paper . . . our paper wasn't delivered yesterday because of the rain . . . I wish it would stop raining. . . ." The associations have to be directly related to the specific object to help you get the meaning.

Combining the Definition and Associations to Arrive at a Meaning

Combining the definition and the to-the-point associations is one of the most effective ways of arriving at the symbol's meaning. The definition provides the objective meaning of the symbol, the association its particular meaning for the dreamer. The definition asks, "What is _____ ?" The association asks, "What meaning does it have for me?" The association usually arises spontaneously as a feeling about a particular object and what role it has played in your life.

Let us look at some examples of how the combination of definitions and to-the-point associations elicit a symbol's meaning. Mary had a dream about George Harrison, but she wasn't sure what it meant. In order to define the symbol, she asked herself, "Who is George Harrison?" She thought of him as "One of the Beatles. He has always been in the background but has recently come into his own." She then asked herself, "What are my own experiences and associations to George Harrison? What part has he played in my life? Is there a part of me that is like him?" She realized that she always liked him but never really noticed him before because he stayed in the background until recently. She also realized that there was a part of herself that felt overlooked, and that she identified a bit with George. When she combined the definition and her to-the-point associations, she got "Someone I have liked but never really noticed until recently; someone who has always been in the background but is now coming into his own." When she asked who this reminded her of, she suddenly realized it represented a part of *her*, that she had always stayed in the background but had recently felt like she was coming into her own. The symbol of George Harrison and this part of her shared common characteristics: they were "in the background," they "recently came into our own," they were both "liked" but "never noticed before."

Note how the symbol and the object it refers to share features that were provided by the definition and the to-the-point associations. A simple way to show this process is with a list like the one that follows:

- *Symbol:* **George Harrison**

- *Definition*: "One of the Beatles; he has always been in the background but now has recently come into his own"

- *To-the-point associations*: "I've always liked him but never noticed him before; there's a part of me that is like him because I have always stayed in the background until now"

- *Combination of definition and to-the-point associations*: Someone who has always been in the background but is now coming into his own, that I have liked but never noticed before

- *Represents:* The part of *me* that has always been in the background and is now coming out into my own

- *Common characteristics:* In background, recently coming into our own, always liked but never noticed before

Often, as in the preceding example, a person can represent different aspects of the dreamer. By defining and describing these "human symbols," you can see which parts of yourself they represent, especially when you dream about people you don't know or who are not currently in your life. In most cases, these people are symbols of the qualities they represent to us. For example, Abraham Lincoln may stand for our honest self, Pablo Picasso our artistic self, and a child our childish self. In other cases, the people we dream about can represent themselves, especially if they are people close to us, for example, spouses. A person can also stand for a class of people; dreaming of an old boyfriend could represent previous relationships, or dreaming of a boss could symbolize authority figures in general. In each case, you have to define the symbol and your own particular association to it to know what it represents.

Sometimes symbols are inanimate objects. Suppose you had a dream about daffodils and wanted to know what they represent. Using the George Harrison chart as a model, you could work toward a definition in this way:

- *Symbol:* **daffodils**

- *Definition:* "Yellow flowers that give me much pleasure"

- *To-the-point associations:* "They are my favorite flowers; yesterday, I saw some and wanted them very badly but couldn't afford to buy them. When I got home, I saw a couple that a neighbor left on my doorstep; I thought it was a miracle, like a wish come true"

- *Combination of definition and to-the-point associations*: Something giving me much pleasure, my favorite, that I wanted badly but couldn't afford, I miraculously found them on my doorstep

- *Represents:* A wish come true of something I want very much but can't afford

- *Common characteristics*: Give me pleasure, my favorite, want badly, can't afford, a wish come true

You will notice that even though an objective definition is asked for, the definition the dreamer provides is often subjective. People frequently provide their own personal associations to a symbol even as they are defining it. So that even though a simple definition of daffodils is "yellow flowers," the dreamer spontaneously adds "that give me much pleasure." Don't censor yourself. When you pay attention to the details of your definitions and associations, you may find these subtle clues to the symbol's meaning.

Animals can also appear in dreams as symbols of parts of yourself, and the words you use to describe them can give you a clue as to what they represent. In this example, a person frequently dreamt of her cat:

- *Symbol:* **my cat**

- *Definition:* "An animal I have had for many years whom I love very much"

- *To-the-point associations:* "She is smart, cuddly, loving, childlike—she is vulnerable but doesn't show that side to anyone. She is like a part of me; I don't know what I'd do without her"

- *Combination of definition and to-the-point associations*: A part of me for many years that I love very much that is smart, cuddly, loving, childlike, vulnerable but doesn't show that side to anyone

- *Represents:* Part of me

- *Common characteristics:* Had for many years, love very much, smart, cuddly, loving, childlike, vulnerable, doesn't show that side to anyone, part of me

You may notice that sometimes the distinction between your definition and the associations blurs. Although a definition is usually more objective and an association more subjective, overlap is common. A clear division is not necessary, because you have to combine the two together to provide clues to the meaning of the symbol. Also notice that these definitions and associations are *unique to the dreamer*. Other people would no doubt describe George Harrison, daffodils, and cats in very different ways. For this reason, nobody can tell you what your dreams mean except yourself. All of these symbols are uniquely yours, derived from your own particular associations and life experiences.

Translating Symbols in a Dream

I'll use the following dream to illustrate how definitions and to-the-point associations help us uncover the meaning of a dream's symbols.

I am trying to rent a car from Alamo Rent-A-Car, but I can't seem to get to it. I keep calling and calling but don't get through. I keep being put on hold. I try to get someone to help me but I can't seem to find anyone in this bureaucratic maze. It's a real mess. I keep waiting and get more and more frustrated. I can't seem to get where I want to so that I can rent the car. I decide it is better to go to Enterprise Rent-A-Car instead. It is more expensive but also more convenient. They pick you up instead of making you try to get through. At least you get where you want to go.

The action in the dream is fairly clear. The dreamer is frustrated waiting to get going and can't seem to find any help. He decides it is better to invest more money for convenience; at least then he will get where he wants to go. The focal points in the dream are the Alamo and the Enterprise. Even though you might think to dismiss these details since they are actual names of different car rental agencies, these symbols turn out to be clues to the dream's meaning. When the dreamer asked himself, "What is the Alamo?" he defined it as "the last fort" and "something that eventually went under." His own associations to the rental company was that it was one he had used in the past. It was inexpensive but bureaucratic. When he asked himself, "What am I reminded of when I think of the last fort, or something I have used in the past that is inexpensive and bureaucratic?" he recognized that Alamo Rent-A-Car symbolized the company he was working for. Nearly everyone he had once worked with had left the company, and he felt like he was left "holding down the fort." The company was slowly going under, just like the Alamo; it was also rather bureaucratic, and he was frustrated because he wasn't getting anywhere in his job. He then defined "Enterprise" as starting his own business and getting out on his own. As the dream said, it was a more expensive route, but it would be more convenient and enable him to get where he wanted to go. The definitions and associations helped Bill recognize what the symbols stood for.

Now you'll see how this process works on a more complicated dream. The following dialogue illustrates how defining and associating to each symbol reveals the underlying meaning:

> I have gone to the top of Squaw Peak with Junie. We are at the very top. It is very narrow at the top. We sit on the ledge, and we have a large pizza and a large bag of chips between us. I spend the whole time trying to figure out how to make room for them without their falling off.

If I were to summarize the dreamer's actions, it would be that she climbed to the top of something and is trying to make room for something without it falling off.

This dream has multiple focal points, so I'll start by asking "What is Squaw Peak?"

> Squaw Peak is a mountain that is very difficult to climb. It is something I have been doing for many months now and something I have always wanted to do. I feel good that I have finally been able to do it.

Then I ask, "What are you reminded of when you think of something that is difficult to climb, that you have been doing for many months now, that you have always wanted to do and feel good that you can finally do it?"

> *Losing forty pounds!*

"And who is Junie?"

> *Junie is a friend of mine who lost a lot of weight at Weight Watchers years ago and has continued to maintain her weight. I admire her. She is my role model, someone who has lost weight and has continued to keep it off.*

"Is there a part of you that is like that?"

I guess that would be the part of me that has lost weight and wants to continue to keep it off.

"What is pizza?"

Pizza is my favorite junk food. So are potato chips. These are the goodies I like to snack on.

"And what comes to mind when you think of your favorite junk foods and your trying to make room for them in the dream?"

That's exactly what I am trying to do, trying to figure out how to eat my favorite junk foods and still maintain my weight loss.

Asking for definitions and associations helped the dreamer recognize what mountain she had climbed in her waking life, and what it was she was trying to make room for on top of that mountain. As you review the different definitions and associations to the symbols, notice how the symbol and its underlying meaning share the same characteristics.

- *Symbol:* **Squaw Peak**

- *Definition:* "A mountain that is very difficult to climb"

- *To-the-point association:* "Something I have been doing for many months and something I have always wanted to do and feel good that I finally did"

- *Represents:* Losing 40 pounds

- *Common characteristics:* Difficult to climb, have been doing for many months, always wanted to do, feel good I did

- *Symbol:* **Junie**

- *Definition:* "A friend of mine who has lost a lot of weight at Weight Watchers years ago and has continued to maintain her weight"

- *To-the-point association:* "I admire her; she is my role model of someone who has lost weight and has continued to keep it off"

- *Represents:* The part of me that has reached her weight goal and wants to maintain it

- *Common characteristics*: Lost weight, maintained it, admire, role model of maintaining weight loss

- *Symbols:* **pizza and chips**

- *Definition:* Junk food

- *To-the-point association:* My favorite, goodies I like to munch on

- *Represent:* Favorite junk food

- *Common characteristics:* Junk food, favorite, like to munch on, trying to make room for

Rewriting the Dream in Everyday Language

Once you understand what each symbol refers to in a dream, you then rewrite the dream story with the new meanings. The new story in the Squaw Peak dream would be as follows:

> I have finally reached my goal of losing 40 pounds and am trying to figure out how to make room for my favorite junk foods and still maintain my weight.

After you rewrite the new story, substituting new meanings for the symbols, you are now ready for the final steps in dream interpretation: understanding the dream's message and applying it to your life.

Summary and Review

Once we summarize the actions, relate them to waking life, and find a focal point, the next step in dream interpretation is to unlock the meaning of each symbol in the dream. By combining the definition of the symbol with your own direct associations to it, you arrive at the link between the symbol and its underlying meaning. The definition is the objective meaning of the symbol, whereas the association—called *to-the-point* to distinguish it from free association—is more subjective. The definition asks: "What is _____?" whereas the association asks "What meaning does _____ have for me?"

- Ask yourself: What is _____?

- What am I reminded of when I think of the words I used to describe ____?

- What are my own associations and experiences with ____?

- What part has _____ played in my life?

- Is there a part of me that is like ____?

After defining and associating to every symbol, you can go to the next step of dream interpretation—rewriting the new dream story, by substituting new meanings for the symbols.

8

Unlocking the
Dream Message

*Dreams are mysterious entities, like messages from
an unknown friend who is caring but objective.
The handwriting and the language are, at times,
obscure, but there is never any doubt as to the
underlying concern for our ultimate welfare.*

—James Hall

"What did you think of the movie you saw last night?" I asked
a friend of mine while we were having lunch together. "I
enjoyed it," she said. "It held my interest the whole time but

afterward I couldn't for the life of me figure out what the point of it was." Unlike movies, which frequently have no purpose other than to entertain us, dreams are usually there for a reason. Every dream is a message from yourself to yourself. The message often comes in a disguised form so that you can choose to look at it or ignore it. If every dream is a story, then the message is the moral, bringing information to your attention so that you can learn from it and act on it. The last steps of dream interpretation are to find the dream's message and apply it to our waking life.

Every Dream Has a Message

At the core of any dream is a message telling you what to do or what not to do. Sometimes the message is a gentle reminder; at other times it is an urgent alarm. You need to pay attention to what you are trying to tell yourself. "What is my dream saying to me? Why am I needing to remind myself of this right now? And most importantly, what do I do with this information? How can I use what I have learned to help me in my daily life?"

> *Many times the message of a
> dream is not hidden.*
>
> —Mark A. Thurston

Some messages are fairly straightforward. Kitty kept having dreams of her boss asking her how a certain project was coming along, a message for her to stop procrastinating and get to work on it. Julie had a straightforward dream a few days before St. Patrick's Day, the first time in years when she was not going to be celebrating with friends. She had a dream about ordering a corned beef sandwich—a message she decided to act on! Thelma's dream, in which she experienced the overpowering grief she felt over the death of a co-worker, made her aware of the sadness she felt and gave her permission to express her emotions.

Some messages are less direct. Dreams frequently tell you what you don't know you know by magnifying the information to bring it to your attention. After a powerful dream, you should ask yourself, "Why do I need to remind myself of this information?" The message is like a map telling you where you need to go and how to get there. The dream tells you, "If you do this, that will happen. If you don't, this will happen." A woman wondering why she has no friends and dreaming that her head is disproportionately large to the rest of her body is telling herself, "If you continue to act big-headed, you will remain friendless." The solution is embedded in the dream: "If you want to have friends, stop having such a big head."

Terry wanted to leave her job to start her own business but kept procrastinating about giving notice. Although she had set a deadline for herself when she would leave her job, she kept postponing it, waiting for the "perfect" time to leave. She had a dream that she was waiting to go to a wedding and kept trying on one outfit after another until it was too late and she missed the wedding. The message was clear: "If you keep waffling and don't make a decision, you will miss your deadline and never get where you want to go." When she still didn't take action, she had another dream that she had a baby who died because she had forgotten about it while taking care of other things. Terry realized that if she kept attending to other matters and neglected her desire to go out on her own, her "baby"—her dream of starting her own business—would die. This powerful message spurred her to give notice and pursue her goals. Dreams can show you the consequences of your actions: "This is what will happen if you continue to postpone leaving your job and starting your own business."

Sometimes you might have dreams that a loved one has died, or you might dream of a very unhappy period in your life. The purpose of these dreams may be to contrast the past with your present situation. You wake up thinking, "Thank God this didn't happen" or "I'm so glad I'm no longer married to _____" or "What a relief that I don't work at my old job any longer." The message in these cases is to remind yourself to appreciate what you have.

Sometimes the message is stated by a person in the dream. For example, Andrea wondered why she was having so many aches and pains that had no physical basis. She had a dream of her father saying to her, "Deal with your anger." This message inspired her to explore the anger underneath her pain and to deal with years of unresolved rage at her father's sudden death in her childhood. By getting to the roots of her current symptoms, she was able to express her anger at being abandoned in a more constructive manner. Her symptoms disappeared. It is not unusual to hear someone giving you advice in a dream. The words can come from a person you respect or even a disembodied voice you hear, as was the case with the person who asked why there was so much evil in the world and heard the message: "Do something about it!"

The message can be conveyed in a phrase or even a line from a song. Anne and her co-workers were going through a difficult transition. She wondered how she could make it through each day at work. She had a dream that she was on a very bumpy airplane ride with fellow passengers and heard the lyric, "a teaspoon of sugar makes the medicine go down." She took this advice to heart, and tried to be sweet to her fellow employees as they took this bumpy ride at work.

More often than not, the advice is not spelled out so clearly. You need to then ask yourself:

- What is this dream trying to teach me?

- What is it bringing to my awareness?

- What am I wishing to tell or remind myself?

Dream Practice

As an exercise, you can review some of the dreams from previous chapters to find the underlying message. I will present some dreams from previous chapters to give you some practice in looking for the dream message. Just as symbols are unique to the dreamer, so too are messages. The moral of the story should be found in relationship to the context, after going through the steps of interpretation. Look at each dream as a story and try to find the moral of the story. Again, for this exercise to be most effective, place a piece of paper over the comments following each dream and write down your answer before reading them. Then go on to the next dream.

> I discover some relatives from a foreign land and talk to them. They start to tell me about their religious beliefs. They say they don't eat sugar and believe that it is evil. They have blinders on their eyes to keep them from making eye contact with each other, because they think that is bad. I think their beliefs are strange and absurd but I doubt myself and don't say anything. We are of the same faith, and I wonder if I'm wrong in my beliefs.

The dreamer meets people whose beliefs he thinks are absurd. Instead of challenging these people, he questions his own beliefs. When he asked himself, "Where in my waking life do I question my beliefs even when I find other beliefs strange or even absurd?" he recognized that he frequently doubted himself and seldom expressed his opinions even against ridiculous opinions. The message of the dream is "Stop doubting yourself and stand up for your beliefs." Even if we don't know what the story refers to, its moral is fairly clear. Once we know what the dream is trying to teach us, we can act on its message—in this case, by speaking up for our beliefs.

> All night long I kept having dreams that I wanted to sing, and I was looking all over for a room where I could sing but I just couldn't find a room.

The dream brings to awareness the dreamer's frustration at not finding a place to do what she wants, and the message may be to continue searching for a place. In this case, the dreamer had been looking for a place where she could express herself and recognized that she needed to continue to do that to stop feeling so frustrated. In her waking life, the dreamer had been feeling frustrated for a long time. She was a highly talented, artistic individual but wasn't able to express herself at work. Singing represented for her a creative outlet as well as "finding her voice." The dream reflected the lack of an outlet for her creativity, and the message for her was that she needed to find that outlet.

> I am floating in a raft. It is very shaky. I have a few belongings, and I'm trying to hold them all together. My umbrella falls off, and I jump down to retrieve it. Then I'm afraid I'm going to drown. I am terrified but I finally make it up without drowning.

The dreamer had been working very hard in her waking life and felt like she was drowning with all the commitments she had. She nearly drowns trying to hold it together in this dream. The message for her was "Don't try so much to hold it all together." It is important that you spell out what you believe the dream is trying to teach you so that you can act on that knowledge. The dreamer in this case decided to cut down on the things she was trying to hold together so that she doesn't feel like she is drowning.

> I'm in a doctor's office, and I'm going to have a baby. The doctor, who is a family practice doctor, is going through everything and doing a good job, showing me slides and ultrasound pictures and quoting statistics. I realize that I am very concerned about the childbirth and need to tell him of my apprehensions, what I want done and so on. I tell him I want to discuss my concerns with him, that I had talked to Dr. X, my gynecologist, in the past, and that it had really helped. The doctor agreed it was important but sort of brushed me off, like we'd get back to that later, at another time. I was disappointed and frustrated because childbirth was my most important concern and I wanted to be as prepared as possible for it, but we never got around to that.

The dreamer's concerns are ignored in this dream, and she ends up feeling disappointed and frustrated. The dreamer had this dream after meeting with a financial counselor who was more interested in dispensing information than in addressing her concerns. He brushed off her questions, and she left the meeting with her anger and frustration. The dream validates for the dreamer that her concerns are not being addressed, and the message for her was to find someone else who will answer her questions. In her case, she decided to go elsewhere.

> I am flying in this dream, and it's a good feeling but I'm afraid I might fall to the ground and crash. I experiment letting go and I fall and fall and then I make myself go up again, and then I fall faster and faster, and I'm afraid to look down but I fall to the ground, and there's a shock absorber on the ground,

and I bounce back and nothing happens to me, and I start flying again.

The dreamer is flying and is afraid of crashing. He experiments with small falls and then falls to the ground but bounces back again. The dreamer had been afraid to let himself go in a relationship, which, like flying, felt good but scary. He had experimented by taking small risks in the relationship but was afraid if he let himself go completely, he would crash and not be able to recover. The dream is saying: "Don't be afraid of letting go. You can bounce back."

> I am back in college, and I feel very overwhelmed. I am enrolled in courses I didn't know I was in, and then I find out that I have some tests to take. I am behind in everything, and I am taking this test which I didn't even know I had to take. The instructor passes out the examination sheets, and by mistake gives me the answer sheet. I am tempted to just write down the answers, but I am honest and give it back to her and continue taking the test.

The dream reflects the dreamer's feeling of being unprepared. The dream could be saying, "Don't take the easy way out even if you feel overwhelmed." In her waking life, the dreamer had been feeling overloaded and unprepared in her search for a new job. She had been offered an easy way out which felt like cheating to her and a compromise of her integrity. She decided not to take advantage of that opportunity, because she wanted to succeed on her own merits.

> I am sitting on a porch railing outside my house, and a man comes selling all kinds of junk, all kinds of gimmicky stuff. I buy some of that stuff even though I don't need it, just because he wanted to sell it.

A woman does things she doesn't want to in order to please other people. The dreamer had been feeling depressed for some time and couldn't put her finger on the cause. Her life was seemingly smooth, and there did not appear to be any glaring obstacles on the horizon. Her dream helped her recognize that her depression was related to her doing things she didn't want to do because others wanted her to. This caused her to accumulate "junk" in the process. The message is not to do things you don't want to do just because someone else wants you to.

> I am in a bowling alley with my friends, and Mick asks me to bowl, and I am just not up to it, and he keeps insisting and insisting until I finally throw the ball, and it is a terrible shot. I get angry and walk off and say, "I am just not ready. I told you I didn't want to bowl."

As in the previous dream, the dreamer does something she doesn't want to because someone else wants her to. The message is also similar: "If you do something you don't want to and are not ready for, you will not do well and get angry about it." The person who had this dream had been feeling pressured by friends to speed up her job search. However, she didn't feel quite ready and preferred to go at her own pace. Her dream confirmed for her that if she sent out résumés and went on interviews because others thought she should rather than when she felt prepared, she would likely not do well and feel resentful afterwards.

Every dream has a lesson to teach you, even if only to confirm what you already know. Even though it is possible to glean several messages from a dream, only you will know what the right one is for you. When I work with people on their dreams, I always ask them to verbalize the message rather than do it for them. Your messages, like your dreams, are uniquely yours.

A dream is your nightly gift to yourself, at times packaged in layers of wrappings you have to peel away to get to its message. Some people are afraid to look inside, seeing it as a Pandora's box instead of the treasure chest it actually is. You need to unwrap these gems of nightly wisdom to discover the message that will help you lead a fuller, richer life.

> *I am interested in the effect dreams may have*
> *upon our lives. I do not care much about what*
> *my living does to my dreams, but I would like to*
> *know how my dreaming shapes (if it does) my life.*
>
> —Jessamyn West

How Can You Apply the Message to Your Waking Life?

The work does not end once you understand your dream's message. In fact, the works is only just beginning. Once you know what your dream means, you need to find out how to use this information. The most important part of dream analysis is putting your dreams into action. "What can I *do* with what I have discovered? How can I make use of it? How will I act on what I have learned?" Often the necessary action is simple and concrete, such as getting a different caterer, switching to a different answering service, or completing a work project. At other times, you have to figure out how to translate the dream message into your waking behavior. For example, if the dream is telling you to stand up for your beliefs, in which situations should you speak up? If the message is that you might drown trying to hold everything together, what concrete actions can you take that would save you from drowning?

What do you need to stop holding on to? What do you need to let go of? If through the dream you recognize that you are doing things you don't want to do just to please others, what specifically do you need to do to stop? Whom do you need to say no to? What *specific, concrete,* and *practical* measures should you take to translate the dream message into your everyday life?

Jeanne's dream, which had her buying junk she didn't need just because someone wanted to sell it, helped her evaluate the areas in her life where she was doing things she didn't want to do just to please others. She decided to discontinue her membership in the gym, which she was going to just because her boyfriend wanted her to go. She also stopped buying so many presents for others. In addition, she made up her mind to turn down several work projects that she had only agreed to do because others wanted her to do. After acting on the dream message in her waking life, she felt much happier.

Candy also decided to apply the dream message to her life. She had been pressured by well-meaning friends to apply for a job, but in her heart, she didn't feel ready for it yet. Her bowling dream gave her permission to wait until she was ready to apply for the job, by reminding her that if she did something she didn't want to and wasn't prepared for, she would do poorly and get angry afterward.

> *More people are afraid of their*
> *dreams than their nightmares.*
>
> —James Grady

You can use your dreams to guide your daily actions. Many times the actions we need to take are spelled out in the dream itself. The dream presents both the problem and the solution, as in this example of a dream related by an attorney I will call Jessica:

> I always have this recurring dream when I'm stressed that I'm enrolled in classes that I didn't know I had enrolled in and it's the end of the semester and I have to take exams and I'm desperately running around since I'm not prepared. This time I had the same dream, but instead of panicking, I decided to go to each advisor and withdraw from the classes with the option to take them later if I want.

Jessica had been feeling overwhelmed trying to juggle work and motherhood demands. The dream told her what to do instead of panicking. She went and talked to each of her law partners and withdrew from some of her commitments with the option of returning to them later if she wished, the same way she had gone to each advisor in her dream and dropped out from the courses.

Making Changes in the Dream

If you have difficulty applying the dream message to your waking life, you can work out the solutions *within the dream* at first and later translate those changes to waking behavior. Although dreams don't always spell out the actions you need to take as clearly as Jessica's dream did, you can usually figure those out for yourself. If you dream for example that you are driving from the back seat, the obvious solution is to get into the driver's seat. If you dream that you can't see well because your headlights aren't working, it follows that you need to turn them on. You can then transfer these solutions to your waking life. Getting into the driver's seat in waking life may mean making your own decisions at work instead of allowing others to make them for you, or telling people what you want instead of having them choose for you. Turning on the headlights in everyday life may mean looking at that boyfriend or girlfriend realistically, instead of shutting your eyes to their behavior.

Jennifer felt trapped in her job and saw no way out of her dilemma in waking life. Her dream of being in a hole reflected her waking feelings. In the dream she found it easy to brainstorm on how she could get out of the hole: she could climb out by herself, she could ask bystanders to give her a hand, she could yell for help, or she could stay calm and recognize that it was only a temporary situation. When she applied these solutions to her work situation, she realized she could stay calm, recognizing that she would eventually get out of there, by looking for another job or asking others for help and support.

> *The dream does not end when we*
> *wake up and write it down.*
> —Mark A. Thurston

Practical Dreaming

Many people have the mistaken notion that dreams are just something fun to talk about. But the *practical* applications of dreams—what we *do* with what we learn from them—are their greatest asset. They can save us headaches, time, and even money as in Catherine's case:

> I dreamt that this business venture I was going into with Bob and his friends was thirty-one million dollars in debt, and we were being investigated by a grand jury. The whole thing was a big mess.

Catherine had in fact been contemplating a business venture with Bob and his friends. At the back of her mind, she had "known" that Bob's other businesses hadn't gone well in the past, that he had a tendency to overspend, and that he had some serious emotional problems; but she had conveniently overlooked these issues because he was a very close friend and she liked him. The dream message was loud and clear: "If you go into business with this guy, you might lose a lot of money." Catherine decided to act on the message and discussed her apprehensions with Bob. He seemed relieved she had brought up the topic and admitted he also had concerns about the business. They were able to work out another arrangement, and Catherine's dream most likely saved her a lot of money as well as a good friendship.

The term "dream" has both positive and negative connotations. You can say something is "just a dream," meaning it is a fantasy or a figment of our imagination—something that has no basis in reality or will never be realized. Or you can talk of a dream as an idea, a hope, a vision that can serve as a goal for you to strive for and make come true. One of the most inspiring phrases in our history is Dr. Martin Luther King Jr.'s "I have a dream . . ." A dream can be a vision of what you want, what you hope to achieve. A dream can be a concrete manifestation of your hopes and aspirations. You can experience vividly the emotions you will feel when you achieve your dreams, or you can use the dream images to inspire you and spur you into action.

Dream on!

> *We grow great by dreams. All big men*
> *are dreamers. They see things in the*
> *soft haze of a spring day or in the red*
> *fire of a long winter's evening.*

—Woodrow Wilson

Summary and Review

The last step in dream interpretation is finding the dream message and applying it to waking life. If every dream is a story, the dream message is the moral of the story, bringing something to our attention so that we can learn from it and act on it. Every dream has a message telling you what to do or what not to do. Once you understand what the dream is trying to teach you, you can use this information to help you improve your everyday life. The practical aspects of applying the dream message to your daily life is probably the most important part of dream analysis.

When you look at your dreams, find the dream message and how you can apply it to your waking life. Ask yourself the following questions:

- What is the message of the dream?

- What is it trying to tell me?

- What is the moral of the story?

- Why do I need to remind myself of this now?

- How can I apply the message to my waking life?

9

The Interpretive
Process: A Case Study

*A dream which is not interpreted is
like a letter which is not read.*

—The Talmud

In the previous chapters, you have seen each of the steps of
dream interpretation examined in detail. This chapter will
summarize and review the entire process by focusing on a single dream to illustrate how it works.

Terry had the following dream:

I was trying to get to a place I wanted to go to—a carnival or something, and I was trying to get my parents to get ready so that we would get there in time. They were procrastinating and taking forever to get ready, and I was feeling very frustrated. I kept waiting and waiting for them so that they would drive me in the little red car they have. At one point my mother was very drunk and lay down in the middle of the road. We were running out of time, and I was afraid we would miss the event. We never got to go because it was getting late. Then suddenly I remembered that I had another car—an old Volvo—that I hadn't used in a long time and that I had forgotten about. I realized I could drive there myself. I went to get the car, and I was pleased I could still drive it but the tires had gone flat. I decided that it was easier to fix it than getting a new car, and I could go where I wanted to.

Before going through the steps, ask yourself if you can figure out what the dream is about.

- *Do I have any idea what the dream is about?*

When Terry asked herself this question, she had no definite idea about the dream's meaning, but she had a vague notion that it may have had something to do with her wishing to make a job change.

Summarize the dreamer's actions in a couple of sentences.

- *What is the dreamer doing?*

- *What is the dreamer feeling? Describe the dream in the third person as though it were a story.*

- *What is the plot or story line?*

- *Try to put the plot into one or two sentences.*

Terry summarized the plot as follows: "The dreamer is frustrated waiting for others to take her where she wants to go and doesn't get there as long as she relies on them. She remembers she has her own vehicle, which can get her where she wants to go, but it needs some work."

Relate the actions to waking life.

- *Where in my waking life am I experiencing the same feelings as in the dream?*

- *Are the actions in the dream similar to any situation in my everyday life?*

Terry asked herself, "Where in my waking life am I feeling frustrated waiting for others to get where I want to go?" She could see the similarities between the actions in the dream and those at her work: she had been feeling quite frustrated at work waiting for her boss to give her new projects; he was procrastinating and getting in the way of her progress, much as her alcoholic mother had frustrated her efforts in the past.

Find the focal point.

- *What stands out for me?*

- *What is not clear?*

- *Is there anything that doesn't fit or doesn't make sense?*

Her mother being drunk stood out for Terry. Although she knew that her mother was an alcoholic, this was the first time she had ever acknowledged it in a dream. Terry could see the similarities between her mother and her boss; analyzing the dream was the first time she consciously acknowledged that he was getting in her way.

Define each symbol in the dream and your own particular associations to it. Use the words in the definition and associations to the symbol to get at its underlying meaning.

- *What is* _____ *(symbol)?*

- *What am I reminded of when I think of the words I used to describe* _____ *?*

- *What are my own associations and experiences with* _____ *?*

- *What part has* _____ *played in my life?*

- *Is there a part of me that is like* _____ *?*

By asking these questions, Terry could understand what each symbol stood for within the context of her current life situation. The different symbols in the dream are carnival, mother, little red car, Volvo, and flat tires. Let's see how this works:

"What is a carnival?"

A carnival is a place I want to go to, a place that is fun, but I wouldn't go there on my own.

"And what am I reminded of when I think of somewhere I want to go to, that is fun and that I keep waiting for others to take me to?"

I want to start new projects that are fun and creative and keep waiting for my boss to give them to me, but he doesn't.

"What is my mother?"

My mother is an alcoholic but this is the first time I have seen her actively drunk. This is the first time I am acknowledging her behavior so graphically and that she deliberately is getting in my path.

"And what comes to mind in the context of my job of someone's behavior deliberately getting in my path that I haven't wanted to acknowledge?"

This is definitely my boss. I keep making excuses for him, just like I used to for my mother. He is deliberately not giving me the projects I want to do and has been giving them to others.

"What is a little red car?"

It's my parents' car, the vehicle they drove us around in when I was a child. I had to rely on them to take me where I wanted to go because the car's not mine—it's theirs.

"And what is the vehicle that I rely on currently to take me places in my career that isn't mine?"

That would be the job itself. I have to rely on my boss to give me the projects I want. I don't work for myself.

"What is a Volvo?"

A Volvo is an old car. It's solid, reliable, and safe. I associate it with the well-to-do, with success.

"What am I reminded of when I think of an old way of getting around that I have forgotten about and haven't used in a long time that is safe, reliable, and successful?"

The analytical and teaching skills I haven't used in this job, my problem-solving skills, my old way of relating that has always been successful and that has gotten me where I want to go.

"What are flat tires?"

They are a part of a car that have temporarily gone flat because of lack of use but they are easily fixable. All you need to do is pump air in them again. It is much easier and less expensive to fill up the tires with air than to get a new car.

"And what has gone flat and needs to have some air pumped in that I haven't used in a long time?"

I guess my skills are rusty and flat, but I can easily brush up on them. They have always been useful in the past.

Rewrite the dream story, using the new meanings:

I am frustrated at work waiting for my boss to give me new projects. He is procrastinating and deliberately blocking my way just as my parents did in the past. I will never do what I want at work as long as I rely on my boss to get me there. I have some safe, solid, reliable skills that have been very useful for me in the past. I had forgotten about them and they are temporarily flat and rusty, but it is easier to brush up on those than to invest in going out on my own. Those skills will get me where I want to go.

Find the dream's message:

- *What is the message of the dream?*

- *What is it trying to tell me?*

- *What is the moral of the story?*

- *Why do I need to remind myself of this right now?*

Terry's dream was telling her that she wouldn't get where she wanted to at work if she waited for her boss to get her there, and reminded her of old skills she had which she had forgotten about that could help her achieve her goals.

Apply the message to your waking life.

- *How can I apply this message to my waking life?*

When Terry asked herself this question, she decided that she would stop waiting for her boss to give her the projects she wanted and instead spend her time brushing up on old skills so that she could do these projects on her own. She eventually left her job and worked on assignments she liked on a consulting basis.

Working with this dream illustrates how to use and integrate the steps to come up with the dream's meaning. In reality, the process is not always as clear-cut or as easy as in this example. I am basically using a left-brain medium to teach a right-bran activity. The left brain is systematic, linear, and follows a formula. The right brain is intuitive and sees the whole picture. Some of the steps may at times seem redundant and unnecessary. They may also not go so clearly or logically in this order. However, the questions are there to serve as guidelines and to bring clarity out of confusion.

Summary and Review

When looking at your dreams, ask yourself if you can figure out what the dream is about before going through it step by step.

- Summarize the dreamer's *actions* in a couple of sentences.

- Relate them to waking life.

- Find the *focal point*.

- *Define* each symbol in the dream and your own particular *associations* to it. Use the words in the definition and associations to the symbol to get at its underlying meaning.

- *Rewrite* the dream story, using the new meanings.

- Find the dream's *message* and how you can apply it to your waking life.

Part 3

Questions and Answers

10

Frequently Asked Questions about Dreams

Was it a vision, or a waking dream?
Fled is that music:—Do I wake or sleep?

—John Keats

Whenever I talk about dreams, I usually get asked the same questions over and over again. What does it mean when you dream that you are dreaming? Can dreams come true? Do dreams foretell the future? In this chapter, I will answer some of the most frequently asked questions about dreams.

Why do I sometimes have the same dream over and over?

"I've had the same dream for as long as I can remember," said Talia. "I am in school, and suddenly I realize that I have exams I have to take that I haven't studied for; I'm late for class, and I feel completely unprepared." Anxiety dreams about being enrolled in classes and not being prepared are quite common and usually appear at times when we are going through a new life situation which brings on anxiety. Talia's recurrent dreams would typically occur whenever she started a new job or a new project. If you have recurring dreams, look at what is happening in your life when you have those dreams to see if there is a pattern linking the recurring dream to a recurring anxiety.

Recurring dreams frequently signify an unresolved conflict. You keep repeating the same dream until you deal with the issue that inspires the dream. Marissa had a recurrent dream that someone was chasing her. She would wake up in terror after these nightmares and be unable to go back to sleep. She tried to figure out what she was running from in her waking life but could not pinpoint the source of her fears. She decided she would confront the person chasing her when the dream presented itself again. The next time she had the dream, instead of running away, she turned around and asked her pursuer who he was and what he wanted from her. The figure turned out to be an old boyfriend who still bounced in and out her life. She kept having the same dream as long as she refused to confront the issues in this "nightmare" relationship, in this case his drug use. Her nightmares stopped when she broke up with him for the last time.

Should I interpret every single dream or just the ones that *seem* meaningful to me? Aren't some dreams just more important than others?

Do not judge a dream's importance immediately. Many dreams that seem to be "about nothing" provide you with valuable information. On the other hand, you do not need to spend hours and hours writing down every single dream you have. As I said earlier in the book, you do not need to make dreaming and recording your dreams a lifetime occupation! If you can remember even one dream a week and use its wisdom in your everyday life, you will be amazed at how helpful it can be.

Why do I have nightmares, and what can I do about them?

Nightmares allow you to discharge emotions and face your daytime fears. When you have a nightmare, you can try to uncover its source in your waking life, just as Marissa did. Then you can deal with the problem either in waking life or in the dream. Research has shown that people can change the endings in their dreams and gain control over their lives in this way. Lottie was molested by her stepfather as a child, and even though he was now in another state and no longer a part of her life, she kept having nightmares about him entering her room. She usually woke up from these dreams very frightened and agitated. She decided she would intervene in her dream and rehearsed what she would do. The next time she had this dream, instead of panicking, she calmly told her stepfather he was never to come into her room again. The nightmares stopped.

Nightmares are also common after a traumatic event, such as a car accident, an earthquake, or a fire. You can relive these events over and over till you come to terms with them.

In this way you can cope with what seems like an insurmountable tragedy, incorporating it into your life so you can move on.

Nightmares are different from sleep terrors. Sleep terrors are sudden arousals with screaming and crying that can last up to an hour. They are quite common in children. Most children outgrow these behaviors by the time they are in their teens. There have been a few rare cases of sleep terrors in adults; in these cases, it is a good idea to be evaluated by a sleep specialist.

When do I need the help of a therapist to understand my dreams?

Although you can learn to understand your dreams by yourself, if you are really blocked over an issue or fear that something very painful may be lurking behind a dream, it could be a good idea to get help from a professional. A therapist can help guide your analysis and perhaps nudge you past your anxiety. A therapist can also help you work through painful revelations exposed by your dream work.

What does it mean when I know I'm dreaming while I'm in the middle of a dream?

This experience is called *lucid dreaming:* when you are in the middle of a dream and realize that you are dreaming. When lucid dreaming occurs, you can control the dream to some extent, just as Marissa and Lottie did. By recognizing you are dreaming, you can change the ending of your dreams. This control is particularly useful for avoiding a recurring nightmare.

Researchers have developed a number of techniques for inspiring lucid dreaming. Before drifting off to sleep, you can tell yourself you are going to be conscious in your dream. You can also ask yourself several times a day: "Am I dreaming or not?" This will get you into the habit so that you will ask your-self the same question when you are in the dream state.

Can dreams foretell the future?

Have you ever had a dream where something happened, and a few days later it seemed to come true. These are called *precognitive dreams*. Laura for example had a dream about an alligator sneaking up and attacking her; a few days later, she was backstabbed by a co-worker. Sally dreamt that her recently widowed father had been having an affair: not long afterwards, he announced his intentions to remarry. Although they may seem miraculous, these types of dreams are not uncommon.

Most precognitive dreams are manifestations of informa-tion you already know at some level. A few years ago, another psychologist and I were going to have a meeting with a physi-cian. The night before the scheduled conference, my colleague dreamt that the physician did not show up to the meeting, which is exactly what happened the next day! Did my col-league have special powers to see the future? Most likely not. When we looked back at the situation, the physician's not showing up to the meeting was fairly predictable. The issues we wanted to discuss at the meeting were conflictual, and this particular man avoided conflict. Had we tried to predict what would happen at the meeting, this would have been the logical consequence. The dream simply put two and two together with the information we already had at our disposal. Many times you "know" the information but it is somewhere in the back of your awareness. The dream brings it to the forefront.

You might have a dream that an accident is about to hap-pen or that your car is going to break down, and then sure enough, these events take place. Magic? Not at all. You may know, for example, that the roads are slippery, that John drinks too much, that the car hasn't had a checkup, and so on.

You can see "an accident waiting to happen," so you are not surprised when John actually smashes up the truck, or the car breaks down. You have "known" all these pieces of information before having the dream. The dream merely spells out the inevitable consequences of facts you already know.

What does it mean when you dream of loved ones who have died?

One of the most comforting aspects of dreams is their ability to help you experience your loved ones again. More than pictures and memories, your dreams allow you to relive precious moments with loved ones and have them constantly near. People who are grieving often look forward to their dreams when for a few moments they can be with a spouse, a parent, or a child again. The dead can live on in dreams long after they die, and dreams of the deceased help the bereaved cope with the stages of grief.

After the death of a loved one, dreams reflect the bereavement process. Studies of bereavement dreams have shown some common elements including the announcement and arrival of the deceased or a message such as "I'm okay," "I'll always love you," or "goodbye." Some dreamers report an embrace and even a dream "gift" symbolizing love, forgiveness, or another emotion, followed by the departure of the loved one, a catharsis that can unleash powerful feelings. These bereavement dreams can go a long way toward healing grief.

Can children use their dreams the same way as adults do?

Children are more apt to remember frightening dreams than pleasant ones. Dreams of being chased, being lost, or failing an exam are more common than happy dreams. Children's dreams, not surprisingly, tend to use childish symbols, such as monsters, ghosts, and cartoon figures.

Children can be taught to understand their dreams much as adults can, and it is not unusual for kids to have a knack for understanding what their dreams mean. Many therapists enjoyed using the techniques with their young friends! Children can learn to look forward to their dreams. As one child said, "It's like the tooth fairy leaving something under your pillow."

Children tend to be concrete and think pictorially so looking at dream stories is quite natural to them. If they have a dream about being terrified of a monster, no interpretation is necessary. Kids can learn to work out the solutions *within the dream* without necessarily understanding what the monster represents. Parents can coach their children to prepare new endings for dreams by asking "What can the child do to make the monster go away?" For example, a mother can tell her son that the next time the monster appears, he can make it disappear (children accept magic much more readily than adults do!). Or your children can come up with their own creative solutions, such as, "Maybe if I pet the monster, I will find out it is really very nice." You may wish to provide young children with a "magic wand" to keep by the bed to chase away bad dreams. The dream object gives them a sense of security and protection and is a concrete tool for coping with bad dreams. Most nightmares in children are a normal part of coping with changes in the children's lives; the bad dreams could be a response to moving to a new neighborhood, having a new sibling, or going to a different school. By teaching your children how to cope with scary dreams, you are teaching them coping skills.

Do medications affect our dreams?

There appear to be two specific groups of medications where a connection to dreaming has been made. Certain categories of antidepressants sometimes cause an increase in recollection of dreams as well as more vividness. People have reported that their dreams are more bright, colorful, or brilliant. The reason for this is not clear, although it may be because these medications reduce the amount of time spent in REM sleep, and the increased recall and intensity may be a rebound effect. Sedatives can also affect dreaming. People taking these medication often report that they stop dreaming. The reason may be that they no longer remember their dreams because they no longer wake up during the night. Many people tend to remember their dreams more clearly when they are woken out of them! Alcohol also has this effect on dream recall.

Where can you get further information on dreams?

In response to the renewed interest in dreams in recent years, the Association for the Study of Dreams was formed. The address is listed below:

ASD
P.O. Box 1600
Vienna, VA 22183

The following books can also provide you with more information on some of the topics covered in this chapter.

- Children's dreams: Patricia Garfield. 1984. *Your Child's Dreams*. New York: Ballantine.

- Dreams about loved ones who are dead: Patricia Garfield. 1996. *Dream Messenger*. New York: Simon &. Schuster.

- Lucid dreaming: Jayne Gackenbach and Jane Bosveld. 1989. *Control Your Dreams*. New York: Harper & Row.

- Using dreams to resolve crisis: Rosalind Cartwright and Lynne Lamberg. 1992. *Crisis Dreaming*. New York: HarperCollins.

Where do you go from here?

I have shown you a method for looking at your dreams and using them in your everyday life. I have presented the material as simply and clearly as I can so that you can immediately begin interpreting your dreams, hearing their messages, and enriching your life. Your dreams are your nightly commentary on the events of the day and a direct line to your inner world. I hope I've helped you tap into that line.

Believe in your dreams!

References

Dement, W. 1960. The effects of dream deprivation. *Science* 131:1705–1707

———. 1964. Experimental dream studies. In *Academy of Psychoanalysis: Science and Psychoanalysis*. Vol. 7. New York: Grune & Stratton.

Dement, W., and N. Kleitman. 1957a. The relation of eye movements during sleep to dream activity: An objective method of the study of dreaming. *Journal of Experimental Psychology* 53:339–346.

———. 1957b. Cyclic variations in EEG during sleep and their relationship to eye movements, body motility and dreaming. *Electroencephaography and Clinical Neurophysiology* 9:673–690.

Gackenbach, Jayne, and Jane Bosveld. 1989. *Control Your Dreams*. New York: Harper & Row.

Gillin, C., and R. Wyatt. 1975. Schizophrenia: Perchance a dream. *International Review of Neurobiolgy* 17:297–342.

Hall, C. S. 1953. *The Meaning of Dreams*. New York: Harper and Brothers.

Hall, C. S., and B. Domhoff. 1963. A ubiquitous sex difference in dreams. *Journal of Abnormal and Social Psychology* 66:278–280.

Koch-Sheras, P. E. 1985. *A re-examination of the difference between men's and women's dreams*. Paper presented at the Second Annual International Conference of the Association for the Study of Dreams, in Charlottesville, Virginia.

Wiess, Lillie. 1992. *Dream Analysis in Psychotherapy*. Needham Heights, Mass.: Allyn and Bacon.

Winget, C., and F. Kapp. 1972. The relationship of the manifest content of dreams to duration of childbirth in primiparae. *Psychosomatic Medicine* 34(2):313–320.

Winget, C., M. Kramer, and R. Whitman. 1972. Dreams and demography. *Canadian Psychiatric Association Journal* 17:203–208.

Zarcone, V., G. Gulevich, T. Pivik, and W. Dement. 1968. Partial REM phase deprivation and schizophrenia. *Archives of General Psychiatry* 18:194–202.

More New Harbinger Titles

THE POWER OF FOCUSING

Takes you step by step through a process of listening to your body, finding words or images to express the feelings that emerge, and letting those messages lead to insights, decisions, and positive change.   *Item POF $12.95*

CLAIMING YOUR CREATIVE SELF

The inspiring stories of thirteen women who were able to keep in touch with their own creative spirit open the door to new definitions of creativity and to the kind of transforming ideas that can change your life.   *Item CYCS $15.95*

GOODBYE GOOD GIRL

The dozens of women whose stories are told in this book confirm that it may be scary to challenge the "good girl" rules, but the results can be astonishing, inspiring, and well worth the struggle.   *Item GGG $12.95*

SIX KEYS TO CREATING THE LIFE YOU DESIRE

Why is the road to satisfaction so difficult to find? This book helps you recognize your core issues and take the steps you need to take to create the life you really desire.   *Item KEY6 $19.95*

FACING 30

A diverse group of women who are either teetering on the brink of thirty or have made it past the big day talk about careers, relationships, the inevitable kid question, and dashed dreams.   *Item F30 $12.95*

Call toll-free 1-800-748-6273 to order. Have your Visa or Mastercard number ready. Or send a check for the titles you want to New Harbinger Publications, 5674 Shattuck Avenue, Oakland, CA 94609. Include $3.80 for the first book and 75¢ for each additional book to cover shipping and handling. (California residents please include appropriate sales tax.) Allow four to six weeks for delivery.

Prices subject to change without notice.

Some Other New Harbinger Self-Help Titles

Claiming Your Creative Self: True Stories from the Everyday Lives of Women, $15.95
Six Keys to Creating the Life You Desire, $19.95
Taking Control of TMJ, $13.95
What You Need to Know About Alzheimer's, $15.95
Winning Against Relapse: A Workbook of Action Plans for Recurring Health and Emotional Problems, $14.95
Facing 30: Women Talk About Constructing a Real Life and Other Scary Rites of Passage, $12.95
The Worry Control Workbook, $15.95
Wanting What You Have: A Self-Discovery Workbook, $18.95
When Perfect Isn't Good Enough: Strategies for Coping with Perfectionism, $13.95
The Endometriosis Survival Guide, $13.95
Earning Your Own Respect: A Handbook of Personal Responsibility, $12.95
High on Stress: A Woman's Guide to Optimizing the Stress in Her Life, $13.95
Infidelity: A Survival Guide, $13.95
Stop Walking on Eggshells, $14.95
Consumer's Guide to Psychiatric Drugs, $16.95
The Fibromyalgia Advocate: Getting the Support You Need to Cope with Fibromyalgia and Myofascial Pain, $18.95
Healing Fear: New Approaches to Overcoming Anxiety, $16.95
Working Anger: Preventing and Resolving Conflict on the Job, $12.95
Sex Smart: How Your Childhood Shaped Your Sexual Life and What to Do About It, $14.95
You Can Free Yourself From Alcohol & Drugs, $13.95
Amongst Ourselves: A Self-Help Guide to Living with Dissociative Identity Disorder, $14.95
Healthy Living with Diabetes, $13.95
Dr. Carl Robinson's Basic Baby Care, $10.95
Better Boundries: Owning and Treasuring Your Life, $13.95
Goodbye Good Girl, $12.95
Being, Belonging, Doing, $10.95
Thoughts & Feelings, Second Edition, $18.95
Depression: How It Happens, How It's Healed, $14.95
Trust After Trauma, $15.95
The Chemotherapy & Radiation Survival Guide, Second Edition, $14.95
Surviving Childhood Cancer, $12.95
The Headache & Neck Pain Workbook, $14.95
Perimenopause, $16.95
The Self-Forgiveness Handbook, $12.95
A Woman's Guide to Overcoming Sexual Fear and Pain, $14.95
Don't Take It Personally, $12.95
Becoming a Wise Parent For Your Grown Child, $12.95
Clear Your Past, Change Your Future, $13.95
Preparing for Surgery, $17.95
The Power of Two, $15.95
It's Not OK Anymore, $13.95
The Daily Relaxer, $12.95
The Body Image Workbook, $17.95
Living with ADD, $17.95
When Anger Hurts Your Kids, $12.95
The Chronic Pain Control Workbook, Second Edition, $17.95
Fibromyalgia & Chronic Myofascial Pain Syndrome, $19.95
Kid Cooperation: How to Stop Yelling, Nagging & Pleading and Get Kids to Cooperate, $13.95
The Stop Smoking Workbook: Your Guide to Healthy Quitting, $17.95
Conquering Carpal Tunnel Syndrome and Other Repetitive Strain Injuries, $17.95
An End to Panic: Breakthrough Techniques for Overcoming Panic Disorder, Second Edition, $18.95
Letting Go of Anger: The 10 Most Common Anger Styles and What to Do About Them, $12.95
Messages: The Communication Skills Workbook, Second Edition, $15.95
Coping With Chronic Fatigue Syndrome: Nine Things You Can Do, $13.95
The Anxiety & Phobia Workbook, Second Edition, $18.95
The Relaxation & Stress Reduction Workbook, Fourth Edition, $17.95
Living Without Depression & Manic Depression: A Workbook for Maintaining Mood Stability, $18.95
Coping With Schizophrenia: A Guide For Families, $15.95
Visualization for Change, Second Edition, $15.95
Angry All the Time: An Emergency Guide to Anger Control, $12.95
Couple Skills: Making Your Relationship Work, $14.95
Self-Esteem, Second Edition, $13.95
I Can't Get Over It, A Handbook for Trauma Survivors, Second Edition, $16.95
Dying of Embarrassment: Help for Social Anxiety and Social Phobia, $13.95
The Depression Workbook: Living With Depression and Manic Depression, $17.95
Men & Grief: A Guide for Men Surviving the Death of a Loved One, $14.95
When Once Is Not Enough: Help for Obsessive Compulsives, $14.95
Beyond Grief: A Guide for Recovering from the Death of a Loved One, $14.95
Hypnosis for Change: A Manual of Proven Techniques, Third Edition, $15.95
When Anger Hurts, $13.95

Prices subject to change without notice.